Learning to Listen, Learning to Teach

Learning to Listen, Learning to Teach

The Power of Dialogue in Educating Adults

JANE VELLA

 Jossey-Bass Publishers
San Francisco

Substantial discounts on bulk quantities of Jossey-Bass books are available to corporations, professional associations, and other organizations. For details and discount information, contact the special sales department at Jossey-Bass Inc., Publishers.
(415) 433-1740; Fax (415) 433-0499.

For sales outside the United States, please contact your local Simon & Schuster International Office.

Jossey-Bass Web address: http://www.josseybass.com

Manufactured in the United States of America on Lyons Falls Pathfinder Tradebook. This paper is acid-free and 100 percent totally chlorine-free.

Library of Congress Cataloging-in-Publication Data
Vella, Jane Kathryn, date.
  Learning to listen, learning to teach : the power of dialogue in educating adults / Jane Vella.
    p.   cm. — (The Jossey-Bass higher and adult education series)
  Includes bibliographical references and index.
  ISBN 1-55542-630-1
  1. Adult learning.   2. Adult education.   3. Teaching.   I. Title.
II. Series.
LC5225.L42V45   1994   93-43176
374—dc20   CIP

FIRST EDITION
HB Printing   10 9 8 7 6 5 4   Code 9427

The Jossey-Bass Higher and Adult Education Series

Consulting Editor
Adult and Continuing Education

Alan B. Knox
University of Wisconsin, Madison

Contents

Foreword

I feel obliged to open this foreword with a warning: You will enjoy reading this book so much that you may wonder if you are learning anything from it. Let me assure you that you will learn more from it than from any textbook written by me (or anyone else). The deep lessons it contains creep up on you and flower into joyful insights.

Jane Vella is one of the most gifted adult educators I have known. She has discovered and mastered the fundamental concepts of adult learning and applies them with flair, imagination, and loving, tender care. But she is more than a gifted teacher—she is also a gifted storyteller. If you find it difficult to put a good novel down at lunchtime, you will find it hard to put this book down for the same reason; you will get caught up in her exciting adventures.

Although I have written eighteen books on the subject myself, I must admit that I was surprised at how much I learned about the theory and practice of adult education from this book. But I am also delighted and rewarded by how much I learned about the people and cultures of lands I have never visited—northern Ethiopia, Tanzania, Indonesia, the Maldives, Nepal, El Salvador, Zimbabwe, Bangladesh. I understand our world better now; I am a more competent global citizen. I have a cadre of new friends: Fatuma in Ethiopia, Auni Makame in Tanzania, Margie Ahnan in Java, Mustafa Hussein in the Maldives, Durga Bahadur Shrestha in Nepal, Mikaeli Okolo in Zambia, Carlos Castillo in El Salvador, Tainie Mudondo in Zimbabwe, Assura Lori in Bangladesh. Jane Vella made them come alive to me.

Have one of the most enjoyable and rewarding trips of your life!

January 1994   Malcolm S. Knowles
                                                  Professor Emeritus
                                                  North Carolina State University

This book is dedicated
with affection
to my two teachers
Lois Harvey
and
Fay Honey Knopp,
who taught me how to listen
and, therefore, how to teach

Preface

We are at a moment in history when sheer demographics are driving us to rethink the current educational paradigms and practices in professional training, in universities, schools, and colleges, in industrial training and community education. How can we teach multitudes on a human scale? How can we reach workers for retraining, senior citizens for varied educational pursuits, youth for the skills and inspiration they need, citizens for the examination of innovative political policies? How can we organize to share the new information and research discoveries virtually pouring from laboratories and libraries? What sure principles can guide us in this vast national and global enterprise? The current concerns about the quality of education urge us to examine the state of the art and the competence of the science and to search for new ways to improve the educational process.

Scope of This Book

This is a book about teaching and learning. As a teacher of adults for more than forty years, I have worked in the United States, Africa, Asia, Latin America, Europe, and the Middle East. Through these experiences of teaching I have gleaned some profound lessons about learning—lessons I will share through a series of stories about teaching events around the world where the power of dialogue in the midst of diversity was effective.

In this book we examine twelve basic principles of adult learning derived from and practiced in diverse settings around the world. Each event related here underscores one key principle. The events I describe show the educational potential of these twelve basic principles. There are many other principles, of course, to guide adult educators. I have fifty more stories to tell.

A significant problem in the education of adults is the perceived distance between teacher and student: between doctor and patient, between lawyer and client, between social worker and troubled parents, between judge and accused, between professor and adult learner. Until this distance is closed, the dialogue limps. The twelve stories in this book demonstrate the efficacy of closing that distance—of searching for means of honest dialogue across cultures, genders, classes, and ages. All of the principles are indeed means to close that gap and develop that dialogue. An adult educator's first task, then, is to discover what mature students want and need to learn. In all of these cases, men and women were learning how to teach adults by practicing the principles that make for dialogue. *Learning to Listen, Learning to Teach* constitutes a dialogue with readers about the power of dialogue in adult learning.

Intended Audience

This book is for all who are concerned about the current educational challenge. If you are an administrator or a professor, a social worker or a health educator, a community education specialist or a physician teaching in a medical school, an entrepreneur or a journalist, in some aspects of your job you are an adult educator. Trainers in industry, literacy workers, nurses doing patient education, hospital and hospice staff welcoming and training volunteers, Peace Corps or National Service trainers and trainees—all can use these principles to enhance the educational work that is an essential part of their jobs. Often our work is with people whose cultural symbols and values are different from our own. These principles show us how concern about using symbols that speak to other cultures—as well as appreciation of diverse sets of values—enhances the potential of learning for teacher and student alike.

Potential of the Book

This is a very personal book about a selection of significant educational experiences that illustrate the power of dialogue. When these twelve principles are honored, learners can respond immediately to the query "How do you know you know?" by saying "We just did it!" Long-term indicators can then be put in place to examine how steadily they are "doing it" in their lives and their work.

How can this book help you learn to use these principles in your own adult education work? We have week-long intensive courses at Jubilee to invite adult educators to learn the principles and practices (we have fifty-two) by using them. Merely reading a description of these twelve principles, and these stories, can be a first step toward practice. The only way to surely learn them is to use them and then examine the immediate and long-term results both for yourself and for the adult learners you serve.

The Approach

The approach of the book is both deductive and inductive. It is deductive as I explain the principles and demonstrate how to use them; it is inductive as I tell the stories and invite the reader's analysis of these same principles in practice. The events took place in twelve very different situations around the world: in Ethiopia and Nepal, in a graduate school in New York and a migrant labor camp in North Carolina, in Tanzania and El Salvador. The cross-cultural nature of the event gives evidence of the usefulness of the focus principle, which transcends cultural differences. The simplicity of the principles shows that they can be applied productively in educational enterprises anywhere. While many principles for effective adult learning were used in each event described, one principle is the focus of each chapter. The book reviews these principles by inviting you to examine them in your active analysis of each event.

In each story I identify the setting for the learning, describe the problem, study the learners and their needs, analyze the educational program and process, and examine one key principle of learning and teaching. I then point out the immediate indicators for evaluation of the learning, as well as the long-range indicators set in place to examine the implication of that learning for life and work. At the end of each chapter there is a challenge to you the reader that invites you to use the principle in some way appropriate to your own situation.

For twenty-two years, as a Maryknoll Sister, I taught in East Africa: Tanzania, Kenya, Zambia. Then, as assistant professor of adult education at North Carolina State University, I taught in Peru and rural North Carolina. Later, as director of Jubilee Popular Education Center, I taught in Haiti, Chile, Zimbabwe, Lesotho, Swaziland, Ghana, and in McGees Crossroads, a hamlet in rural North Carolina where migrant Haitian workers strove valiantly to learn English. As director of training for Save the Children, I taught in El Salvador, Honduras, Sudan, Korea, Ethiopia, Indonesia, Timor, Guatemala, Ecuador, Cyprus, Jordan, Bangladesh, Sri Lanka, and the Maldives, as well as on the American Indian reservations of Arizona and New Mexico. Through this rich, international experience I have discovered many principles for effective adult learning. They were recognized as effective in the fields of Ethiopia during the drought, on the islands of the Maldives, on the back porch of a migrant camp in North Carolina, in the villages of Tanzania. While these principles are perhaps familiar to you, my own particular interpretation of each one and the unique applications demonstrated in the stories are a function of the international experience. I have discovered that it does make a difference to use problem-based learning—what we call popular education.

To do this educational work, I stand on the shoulders of many educators who are my teachers: Paulo Freire of Brazil, Humberto Maturana of Chile, Julius Nyerere of Tanzania, Malcolm Knowles, Alan Knox, and Carl Rogers of the United States, Kurt Lewin of Germany and the United States, and Carl Jung of Switzerland.

These researchers and scholars taught me from their books; the thousands of folks I have met around the world taught me from their lives.

Overview of the Contents

Part One comprises two chapters. In Chapter One we examine twelve principles that assure dialogue and effective learning. Chapter Two shows how these twelve principles can be applied to ensure the effectiveness of an adult learning event.

The next twelve chapters, Part Two of the book, offer specific applications of the principles by describing twelve actual events. Chapter Three takes place in Ethiopia during the extreme time of famine and drought, in the mountains north of Addis Ababa. Fatuma, the heroine of our tale, helps us realize how important it is to do a comprehensive *needs assessment* before beginning a program. The implementation of this principle is the heart of that story and actually made the program work. Chapter Four tells of a development project in Tanzania near Lake Victoria, where the principle of *safety* was not used wisely enough to include an outsider. This example reinforces the need for safety for both adult learners and their teachers. Chapter Five describes how the *relationship* between teacher and learner informed and enhanced a one-on-one adult learning situation with an Indonesian physician, a Jubilee Fellow, working closely with fellow educators to learn the rudiments of popular education. This chapter demonstrates the cultural implications of such a learning relationship.

Chapter Six takes place in rural North Carolina at a migrant labor camp where I taught English as a second language for a summer. It teaches the principles of *sequence and reinforcement*, showing how they enabled the Haitian migrant workers to grasp a great deal more than language skills. Chapter Seven tells of a long training course with development workers in the Maldives, an island nation in the Indian Ocean. The principle taught here is *praxis*: doing what you are learning. The anecdotes in this story demonstrate the value of praxis and show a variety of practices that implement the principle. Chapter Eight describes an adult education event in the Himalayan mountains of Nepal, demonstrating how learners develop when they are sure of themselves as *subjects* or decision makers in their own learning.

Chapter Nine shows how adult learning can be made effective through the use of multilevel approaches—*cognitive, affective, and psychomotor: ideas, feelings, and actions*—in the learning task. The story takes place in a church community in Zambia. The adult learners were deeply moved and showed how much they had learned because we used this principle in the design of the program. Chapter Ten takes place in El Salvador, where the principle of *immediacy* is manifest in all aspects of the event. It was a critical time in the history of the community development program and, indeed, of the country. Immediacy made for effective learning by all involved. Chapter Eleven moves to a graduate school in New York where the principle of *role and role development* helped professors adopt a new way of teaching. This group of learners, graduate school professors, was a long way from the islands of the Maldives or the Himalayan mountains. Even so, the same principles worked with them.

Chapter Twelve moves back to Africa—to Zimbabwe immediately after independence—where we see how the principle of *teamwork* enabled soldiers of the former army of liberation to transform themselves into literacy teachers for the new nation. They could not have learned what they learned in the short time available without working efficiently in teams. Chapter Thirteen takes place in eastern North Carolina, where we see the importance of *engagement* for the learning and development of critical thinking in a community. The final story, Chapter Fourteen, takes us to an international hospital in Bangladesh where the principle of *accountability* enabled doctors to learn a new way of teaching.

Part Three concludes the book, with two chapters. Chapter Fifteen, a summary and synthesis, offers another example of how the twelve principles work together. Chapter Sixteen explains how this book can make a difference in planning, teaching, and evaluating community education.

The reader is invited to take part in each of these stories through the design challenge at the end of each chapter, where the key principle is presented as a possibility for application in your own educational work. Each story is replete with applications of the key principle of the story as well as all the other principles of dialogue. A comprehensive reference section of materials relevant to this educational approach completes the book.

Acknowledgments

I could not have completed this work without the devoted and efficient support of my partner in Jubilee, my sister, Joan Vella. My long-term mentors, Malcolm Knowles and Paulo Freire, offered encouragement and assistance when I most needed it. Five patient readers offered invaluable suggestions: Karen Bartlett and Paula Berardinelli of Raleigh, Alan Knox of Wisconsin, John Peters of Tennessee, and Budd Hall of Toronto. The encouragement and support of the editors at Jossey-Bass have made this a challenging and pleasant learning experience that has made a world of difference, not only to the quality of this book, but also to my own development as teacher and learner.

Raleigh, North Carolina   Jane Vella
January 1994

The Author

Jane Vella is president of Jubilee Popular Education Center in Raleigh, North Carolina, and is an adjunct professor at the School of Public Health, University of North Carolina, Chapel Hill. She received her B.A. degree (1955) from Rogers College in New York, her M.A. degree (1965) from Fordham University, and her Ed.D. degree (1978) from the University of Massachusetts, Amherst.

Vella has worked in community education in Africa, Asia, North and South America, and Europe since 1955. She has designed and led community education and staff development programs in more than forty countries around the world. During her tenure at Save the Children (US), she did the field research that resulted in the publication of her book *Learning to Teach* (1989).

PART ONE:

A Proven Approach to Teaching Adults

1

Twelve Principles for Effective Adult Learning

A principle, the philosopher tells us, is the beginning of an action. As I begin the design of a course, or a seminar, or a workshop for adult learners, I can make informed decisions that will work for these learners by referring to certain educational principles. And most of these principles apply across cultures. In this first chapter, we will examine twelve basic principles that are deeply interconnected. While these principles have been tested in community education settings, I hold that they can offer insight into the educational processes for teachers and professors in the formal system. As we shall see in the case studies, these principles have been proven to work under diverse and difficult conditions.

One basic assumption in all this is that adult learning is best achieved in dialogue. *Dia* means "between"; *logos* means "word." Hence, *dia* + *logue* = the word between us. The approach to adult learning based on these principles holds that adults have enough life experience to be in dialogue with any teacher, about any subject, and will learn new knowledge or attitudes or skills best in relation to that life experience (Knowles, 1970). All twelve principles are ways to begin and maintain and nurture the dialogue:

- Needs assessment: participation of the learners in naming what is to be learned

- Safety in the environment and the process
- A sound relationship between teacher and learner for learning and development
- Careful attention to sequence of content and reinforcement
- Praxis: action with reflection or learning by doing
- Respect for learners as subjects of their own learning
- Cognitive, affective, and psychomotor aspects: ideas, feelings, actions
- Immediacy of the learning
- Clear roles and role development
- Teamwork: using small groups
- Engagement of the learners in what they are learning
- Accountability: how do they know they know?

Principle 1: Needs Assessment

Doing an adequate needs assessment is a basic principle of adult learning, which honors the fact that while people may register for the same program they all come with different experience and differing expectations. How can we discover what the group really needs to learn, what they already know, what aspects of the course that we have designed really fit their situations? Listening to learners' wants and needs helps to shape a program that has immediate usefulness to adults.

Thomas Hutchinson of the University of Massachusetts, Amherst (1978), offers a useful question for needs assessment: Who needs what as defined by whom? The WWW question—*who* as needers; *what* as needs; *whom* as definers—reveals the political issues involved in preparing a course for adult learners. Who decides? Who are, indeed, the subjects, the decision makers, of this course? Is it the teacher? Is it the learners?

I cannot teach what I do not know. I have the issues and

knowledge sets that I call priorities and, of course, I want to teach them first. The adult learners, however, can decide what is to be taught, as well. They will vote with their feet if the course does not meet their needs. They will simply walk out. As teacher, I need to discover what they know and what they think they need or want to know. How do I hold these opposites, listen to these learners as well as their managers or their clients, and then design a course that meets their needs?

This listening effort is what we call a needs assessment. It is both a practice and a principle of adult learning. Paulo Freire (1970) refers to it as thematic analysis, a way of listening to the themes of a group—the issues that are vital to people. When adult learners are bored or indifferent, it means their themes have been neglected in planning the course. Motivation is magically enhanced, however, when we teach them about their own themes. People are naturally excited to learn anything that helps them understand their own themes, their own lives.

Myles Horton, founder of the Highlander School in Tennessee, discovered how well the police in that state understood this principle in the 1930s. As a young man he was arrested and indicted for "having gone to the miners, listened to them and then having gone back and taught them what you heard" (Adams, 1975, p. 33). In fact he was indicted for having done a needs assessment. "Listening to them" is the operative phrase here. How do we listen to adult learners before we design a course for them, so that their themes are heard and respected? Today, we can use faxes and telephone conversations, we can use a small focus group to review the plan of a course or workshop or training, we can do a survey. A well-distributed sample of even 10 percent of the group can give you important information for your design.

A colleague of mine, Dr. Paula Berardinelli, doing training in time management skills with a group of secretaries at a major industry, sent a number of them the draft program for the training a month before the event. She indicated that she would be calling them for a ten-minute conversation on a specified day. When she spoke with them, one by one, she heard a similar set of themes about their work. She also heard, over and over, how delighted they were by her call. They cited many incidents she could use in the training—as stories for analysis, praxis material for reflection—and helped her understand some of the unspoken variables they were working with. The result was a course that was accountable to the industry and to the adult learners, who knew themselves to be subjects in a healthy relationship with the teacher. Although she spoke with only one-tenth of the group, the entire unit had heard of her needs assessment and were prepared at the outset of the day to offer their ideas spontaneously and creatively. Virtually all of the secretaries said this had never happened to them before.

The case I cite in Chapter Three from the horrors of the drought-swept Ethiopian mountains is an extreme example of the need for a needs assessment. I cannot imagine what might have occurred there with those young teachers and Fatuma if I had not used Hutchinson's WWW principle: *who* needed *what* as defined by *whom*.

Principle 2: Safety

Safety is a principle linked to respect for learners as subjects of their own learning. But it has an added connotation. It means that the design of learning tasks, the atmosphere in the room, and the very design of small groups and materials convey to the adult learners that this experience will work for them. Safety does not obviate the natural challenge of learning new concepts, skills, or attitudes. Safety does not take away any of the hard work involved in learning. Should learning be designed to be challenging or to be safe? The answer is yes! Carl Jung, Swiss psychiatrist and teacher, suggests a pattern for addressing such dilemmas: hold the opposites!

Safety is a principle that guides the teacher's hand throughout the planning, during the needs assessment, in the first moments of the course. The principle of safety enables the teacher to create an inviting setting for adult learners. People have shown that they are not only willing but ready and eager to learn when they feel safe in the learning environment. What creates this feeling of safety?

First: trust in the competence of the design as well as the teacher enables the learners to feel safe. It is important to make your experience and competence clear—either through written materials that learners have read beforehand or through introductory words with them. This is a natural way to make learners feel safe and confident in their teacher.

Second: trust in the feasibility of the objectives, and in their relevance, makes learners feel safe. It is important not only to review the objectives with the group but also to point out how these aims have been established through a listening activity with the learners that we call the needs assessment. Point out that the objectives are empirically based, since they have been successfully used in similar sessions, and show how the objectives are flexible, how they can change to fit this particular group. Indeed, physical manifestations of a feeling of safety appear after such a review of objectives: people relax, smile, start talking more freely to one another.

Third: allowing small groups to find their voices enhances the possibility of safety. When asking learners their own expectations, hopes, or fears about a learning event, or norms they want to see established in the large group, invite them to work in small groups. Four learners at a table large enough for their materials, small enough for them to feel included, provides physical and social safety for learners. You can hear the difference in the room as learners find their voices in the small group.

Fourth: trust in the sequence of activities builds safety. Beginning with simple, clear, and relatively easy tasks before advancing to more complex and more difficult ones can give learners a sense of safety so they can take on the harder tasks with assurance.

Fifth: realization that the environment is nonjudgmental assures safety. Affirmation of every offering from every learner, as well as lavish affirmation of efforts and products of learning tasks, can create a sense of safety that invites creativity and spontaneity in dealing with new concepts, skills, and attitudes. Affirming is one of the basic tasks of every teacher. As we affirm what we hear, we invite learners to use the power they were born with as subjects of their own lives. Teachers do not empower adult learners; they encourage the use of the power that learners were born with.

How can safety be endangered? The fatal "plop"—when an adult learner says something in a group, only to have the words hit the floor with a resounding "plop," without affirmation, without even recognition that she has spoken, with the teacher proceeding as if nothing had been said—is a great way to destroy safety in the classroom. Safety in this case is destroyed not only for the person who spoke but for all in the room. Just as you can see the physical manifestations as learners feel safer and safer, you can observe definite physical manifestations after such a "plop." You can watch the energy draining out of learners. The rise and fall of learners' energy is an accurate indicator of their sense of safety. In the situation in Tanzania (Chapter Four), we see how safety was desperately needed to keep a gifted Muslim teacher working with a Christian community—and how the absence of safety destroyed the potential of teacher and learners alike.

Principle 3: Sound Relationships

Sound relationships for learning involve respect, safety, open communication, listening, and humility. The initial meeting between teacher and learner has to demonstrate the sense of inquiry and curiosity felt by the teacher. When doing a needs assessment, using either focus groups or telephone surveys, the teacher can discover specific personal or group learning needs. Such a dialogue about learners' expectations is a way to confirm our perception of their needs or to amend it. Again, the learners are immediately in the position of subjects, deciding what they want to tell us, feeling safe enough to share their true feelings. A manager of a nonprofit organization in Boston, responding to a telephone call inviting him to name his unique learning needs for an upcoming management seminar, said: "I am honored by this call. It's the first time anyone ever asked me what I wanted or needed to learn!" He was about to attend the seminar at Tufts University. Imagine the relationship that was established between him and the professor via that simple phone call.

This relationship must transcend personal likes and dislikes. If a teacher feels a strong dislike for an adult learner, she knows she must be even more careful about showing respect, affirming, and listening carefully. When the teacher fails to show respect or fails to affirm a learner in a group or allows the fatal "plop," the whole group begins to doubt the learning relationship and often manifests anger, fear, and disappointment. Nothing can diminish the importance of the relationship for learning: respect, affirmation, listening. The example in Chapter Five of Dr. Margie Ahnan from Indonesia shows how powerful this relationship can be in getting an adult learner to stretch beyond himself and grow in the knowledge, skills, and attitudes he needs.

Principle 4: Sequence and Reinforcement

Sequence and reinforcement are vital but often overlooked as principles of adult learning. We have an axiom: do it 1,142 times and you have learned it! Those 1,142 times should be properly sequenced: from easy to difficult, from simple to complex. This seems such a basic concept. Failing to honor it, however, can lead to people dropping out of courses, people acting out anger, fear, and disappointment, adults believing they cannot learn.

Sequence means the programming of knowledge, skills, and attitudes in an order that goes from simple to complex and from group-supported to solo efforts. Learning tasks can be readily examined for sequence. The manifestations of safety and enthusiasm and readiness to achieve indicate that sequence is being honored. When you, as teacher, see fear, confusion, reluctance to try in the learner, test the sequence of the learning task. You may find you have not honored their need for small steps between tasks and their need for reinforcement.

Reinforcement means the repetition of facts, skills, and attitudes in diverse, engaging, and interesting ways until they are learned. The design of reinforcement in adult learning is the job of the teacher. Although the adults may do their own reinforcement through practical work and study, our designs, if they are to be accountable, must carry adequate reinforcement within them to assure learning.

This is the heart of the matter. In adult learning situations—in industry, community, family, or in learning sessions for personal advancement—the teacher is accountable for a design that works for the learners there and then. In formal school situations, young students are "taught" and then admonished to go home and learn what they have been taught so they can pass the test at the end of the course. They are accountable to the teacher. In adult learning, the accountability is mutual. Busy managers attending a course on strategic planning, busy community people trying to learn how to organize for new legislation, families trying to learn how to communicate more effectively, individuals learning how to use a new word processing program—all need an accountable design and an accountable teacher to provide the necessary sequence and reinforcement tasks. They will do the work that enables them ultimately to know that they know. It is our job as designers of adult learning and teachers of adults to assure that the principle of sequence and adequate reinforcement is honored within the learning program.

Suppose a group of adult learners comes together to study opera. They are newcomers to the art. A focus group with three of them has shown that they want to know something of the development of the genre, but above all they want to learn how to listen to an opera for maximum enjoyment and intelligent response. The design assures sequence and adequate reinforcement by taking a familiar opera like Puccini's *Madama Butterfly* and listening for five or six basic forms. The learning tasks would move from basic recognition of forms—That's an aria! That's recitativo!—to a judgment on the quality of the music, using new terms heard in demonstrations by the teacher. The teacher listens to the adult learners and changes learning tasks to meet their needs for reinforcement. If the task is too difficult for most of the learners, it must be changed. This is what we mean by learning as dialogue. This puts the adult learners in the position of subjects—decision makers as to what tasks are appropriate—in a healthy relationship with the teacher, who is not afraid to ask: "How does this task feel at this moment?" The example of building sequence and adequate reinforcement into a program preparing teachers to teach English as a second language and literacy skills to migrant workers in North Carolina (Chapter Six) demonstrates the importance of this principle.

Principle 5: Praxis

Praxis is a Greek word that means action with reflection. There is little doubt among educators that doing is the way adults learn anything: concepts, skills, or attitudes. Praxis is doing with built-in reflection. It is a beautiful dance of inductive and deductive forms of learning. As we know, inductive learning proceeds from the particular to the general whereas deductive learning moves from the general principle to the particular situation. Praxis can be used in teaching knowledge, skills, and attitudes as learners do something with the new knowledge, practice the new skills and attitudes, and then reflect on what they have just done.

Praxis is an ongoing process, of course. We use it in our daily lives all the time as we do something, reflect on its implications, and change. In a learning situation, we use case studies inviting description, analysis, application, and implementation of new learning—that is, praxis. When we set a group of adults to practicing a skill and invite them, as subjects, to analyze the quality of their practice, that moves practice to praxis.

Another way of seeing praxis is as a process: doing–reflecting–deciding–changing–new doing. When posing a problem to learners through a case study, video, or story, we use open questions to invite praxis. These four open questions move through these steps:

1. What do you see happening here? (description)
2. Why do you think it is happening? (analysis)
3. When it happens in your situation, what problems does it cause? (application)
4. What can we do about it? (implementation)

Our job as designers of adult learning is to design learning materials and set learning tasks in appropriate sequence and with adequate reinforcement. These tasks give people the chance to practice new ideas or skills or attitudes and immediately to reflect on them, making practice praxis.

The story of Mustafa Hussein and his community development colleagues (Chapter Seven), in the program in the Maldives, offers specific examples of praxis. Their learning was a result not only of their action in the villages but of quiet and reflection after that action.

Principle 6: Respect for Learners

Regarding the learners as *subjects* of their own learning is a principle that involves the recognition that adults are in fact decision makers in a large part of their lives. Healthy adults desire to be subjects—decision makers—and resist being treated as objects, something that can be used by someone. In this approach to learning, we assume that people are not designed to be used by others. Adults as subjects of their own learning need to know that, insofar as possible, they themselves decide what occurs in the learning event.

The dialogue of learning is between two adult subjects: teacher and student. For example, new content in a course can be shown to the learners with the question: "What else do you feel you need to learn about this topic?" This approach makes the content an open system inviting the critical analysis, editing, and additions of adult learners. Here are some ways to invite learners to be subjects of their own learning.

When teaching something predetermined, such as the facts of national history, we can always offer an open question that provides the vital element of choice: "Here are the dates of important events in the history of this nation. Which one seems the most important to you in terms of reaching independence? Why did you choose that date?" Before teaching the steps in a new computer program, the teacher can ask: "Which of these steps seems like it is going to be most useful to you in your work?" This question invites both teacher and learners to approach the learning as subjects. In teaching adults the personnel processes of an organization in a job-related orientation program, the instructor can begin by asking an open question: "Here is our company process for taking sick leave. Look at all the steps. Which ones would be difficult for you? How does this process differ from the process you knew in another organization you worked for?"

In approaching adult learners as subjects, the teacher must distinguish between their suggestions and their decisions. This is sometimes called the distinction between a consultative voice (a suggestion) and a deliberative voice (a decision). Engaging adults in their own learning means engaging them as subjects of that learning. As far as possible, they make decisions on what and how they will learn. At times they offer suggestions; at times they make decisions. It is essential that we are clear about the difference.

The difference between being perceived as an object and being perceived as the subject of one's own learning is powerful. How can we offer adult learners as many opportunities for choice as possible? One practical guide is: Don't ever do what the learner can do; don't ever decide what the learner can decide. As we shall see when we examine the principle of engagement, the learning is in the doing and the deciding. Teachers must be careful not to steal that learning opportunity from the adult learner. The example in Nepal (Chapter Eight) points out how Durga's feeling himself the subject of his learning enhanced his development of the knowledge, skills, and attitudes being taught. This principle, as you will see, simply acknowledges the uniqueness and human potential of the learners as decision makers in their own learning.

What happens if we recognize learners as subjects? It can mean a radical change in our way of teaching. It can lead to radical changes in the effect of teaching: fewer dropouts, for example, as learners feel themselves respected and important decision makers or subjects of their own learning. It can mean more measurable results of the learning process, as learners know they know because they have chosen to do what they are learning. It can mean better use of financial and human resources, as adult learners practice making healthy decisions in the learning process. Paulo Freire, Brazilian educator, entitled one of his books *Education as the Practice of Freedom*. Inviting learners to be subjects of their own learning is indeed the practice of freedom.

Principle 7: Ideas, Feelings, Actions

Learning with the mind, emotions, and muscles—or attention to the cognitive/affective/psychomotor aspects of adult learning—is a vital principle that is often neglected. When the formalities of teaching/learning from the classroom and university take over without reflection, adult learners can be faced with a mass of cognitive matter: information, data, and facts that may seem impossible to comprehend or learn. When taking my first computer course, I had the personal experience of being deluged with facts about the history and emerging complexity of computers. I simply wanted to know how to use one. The mass of information frightened me off and I became another statistic: another adult learner who began a course and then dropped out.

Using the principle that there are three aspects of learning—ideas (cognitive), feelings (affective), and actions (psychomotor)—we can prevent that initial freezing fear at the outset of a new adult learning process. We know that most learning involves more than cognitive material (ideas and concepts). It involves feeling something about the concepts (emotions) and doing something (actions). Whether I am learning the concept of stakeholders in strategic planning, or the skill of playing the piano, or the attitude of confidence when addressing an audience, I need to consider all three aspects: cognitive, affective, psychomotor.

The concept of preparing an agenda for a meeting, for example, certainly has affective overtones for someone learning how to have an effective meeting. Who is deciding the agenda? As soon as we consider the political implications of making an agenda and preparing a meeting, we have to practice doing it. The more frequently I design an agenda, the more fully I grasp the concept. In this example, to learn the idea I have used a cognitive approach (defining an agenda), a psychomotor approach (designing it), and an affective approach (considering the implications of my preparation for the others in the meeting). Kurt Lewin taught in 1951 that little substantive learning takes place without involving something of all three aspects.

The formal approaches to learning often assume that the cognitive aspect is everything. Joseph Campbell (1988, p. 142) has a startling insight: "The brain thinks it is running the show. It isn't really. It is a peripheral organ, secondary at best!" In the Zambian example (Chapter Nine), church leaders who have struggled long and hard with the concept of equality, and who preach it, got a chance to feel it and do something with it. The results, to say the least, are interesting. The design challenge in that chapter invites you to study your own educational projects in terms of cognitive, affective, and psychomotor possibilities (ideas, feelings, and actions).

Principle 8: Immediacy

Most recent research recognizes that adult learners need to see the immediate usefulness of new learning: the skills, knowledge, or attitudes they are working to acquire. Most adults do not have time to waste. We want to spend our time studying that which will make a difference now. We are willing to work in an appropriate sequence, and we recognize the need for reinforcement, but we want to see something in hand as soon as possible. This principle can guide adult educators so they will be able to hold on to that large percentage of adult learners who start a course and then decide to give it up. Often, there are no immediate results to keep them on board for the entire course.

How does this principle translate into practice? In designing a time management course for middle managers at a large factory, a teacher uses the principle of immediacy by designing three short sessions instead of a day-long course. She makes sure the managers have one particular skill to practice at their posts in between these short sessions. When that skill makes a difference in the management of their usually frenetic and pressured activities, they gain confidence in the course, in the teacher, and in their own learning ability. A question we can offer at the end of each learning session is: "How can you use this new skill most effectively?" So, again as subjects, they decide on the significance and application of the new skill.

The principle of immediacy helped the teacher to decide how to organize the sessions in that short course. This offers an immediate example of what we mean by a principle: the beginning of an action. We know how to begin that action, design that course, because of this simple principle of immediacy. The principle of honoring learners as subjects would have us asking the learners after the three short sessions: "How else could we have organized the time in this time management course? Let's use the very principles we've just learned to redesign this course!" That is using the principle of reinforcement. As we develop skills in the use of all twelve principles, we shall see how deeply intertwined they are. You can hardly use one without using all the others.

In the war-torn streets of the little town of Due Arroyo in El Salvador (Chapter Ten), the community organizers studying the principles and practices of popular education had more than enough immediacy. The story shows how they applied what they were learning wisely enough to save their lives—and mine.

Principle 9: Clear Roles

Another vital principle of adult learning is recognition of the impact of clear roles in the communication between learner and teacher. As Paulo Freire put it in conversation with us one evening: "Only the student can name the moment of the death of the professor." That is, a teacher can be intent upon a dialogue with an adult learner, but if the learner sees the teacher as "the professor" with whom there is no disagreement, no questioning, no challenge, the dialogue is dead in the water. Adult students need reinforcement of the human equity between teacher and student. It takes time for adults to see themselves and the teacher in a new role.

In rural African villages, my colleague and I, two women, spent a lot of time before teaching our leadership course walking around, holding the babies, talking to the mothers. We swapped recipes in their kitchens and spent time watching them weave palm before asking to try it ourselves. The women always enjoyed our brave and clumsy efforts and patiently tried to demonstrate the skill again and again. When we started to teach them, we had a significant new role in the eyes of these village leaders.

Before beginning a recent program with a national literacy organization, I spent time asking all the senior managers about their most recent discoveries in literacy education. "Dr. Vella" was soon transformed into "Jane"—a fellow searcher for ways to teach literacy who was interested in their work and their discoveries. When we finally started the program, I felt their respect for my questions and interest. I had included myself somehow in their work by making those telephone calls and simply asking: "What's new? What should I know about your present work?" My needs assessment established some equity in our roles.

Role is a delicate cultural issue. In some situations around the world—as a woman in a Muslim country, for example—it was vital to be "Dr. Vella" the whole time. In other situations, a first-name basis moved us toward dialogue. What's in a name? The ancient role of dominator, incompatible with this effort at dialogue, may sometimes be connoted by titles and rank. But we wish to move adults to learn together in dialogue. Whatever impedes that dialogue must be courageously addressed and eradicated. Whatever enables that dialogue must be fearlessly nurtured and used. Accessibility is an issue here. If the teacher's role does not lend itself to dialogue, learners will not seek her out. If the teacher is committed to a role that moves both toward dialogue, she will make sure there is time for dialogue both inside and outside the classroom. Time spent with learners at a party, or at a dinner, in a different role, makes a big difference in their freedom to ask the disturbing question, to disagree with a point, to venture a novel opinion.

Role clarification and the move toward dialogue are never a cosmetic issue: they are both a matter of the heart and the heart of the matter. A graduate student recently suggested that another name for this principle is humility. In the graduate school of theology in New York (Chapter Eleven), we see professional men and women struggling toward dialogue, examining their roles with learners and with one another. Ironically, their work is to share the word from their religious tradition. This story tells how they found new meaning in the concept of *dia* + *logos*, the word between us, as they found new roles and new relationships with their graduate students and with one another in this new way of teaching.

Principle 10: Teamwork

Teamwork is itself both a process and a principle. Teams provide, in the adult learning experience, a quality of safety that is effective and helpful. The assurance of safety and shared responsibility available in teams has always proved welcome, no matter what the cultural setting. Teamwork cannot be taken for granted. After a careful needs assessment, the teacher must take advice about the formation of teams. People can be invited to work with friends when possible. This provides safety for undertaking the difficult tasks. The concept of "optimal field" works for us here. An optimal field is one designed for everyone to gain as much as possible—where we design for a win/win situation, including everything in the field that makes for success. If you, as teacher, see negative energy between people, keep them on separate teams. That negative energy can destroy the learning effort. Respecting people as subjects, try to have people choose their own teams as often as possible, especially when the learning task is complex and difficult. You can set up arbitrary teams at the beginning of a course and then have people form work teams for themselves, choosing whom they wish to work with. At times, gender or age or race are serious considerations. It is the teacher who has the deciding vote on teams if such issues seem to divide the learning group. Dealing with the issue of the divisive factor can become a part of the learning process.

All too often we hear people in educational settings say: "When we get back to the real world . . ." Teams *are* the real world. Team efforts in a learning situation are not vicarious and they are not contrived. What happens in the team is often what is happening every day. As adult educators we must remember that feelings are never simulated. If an adult feels overwhelmed and excluded in a small group of people, those feelings are real. That adult will act out of those feelings throughout the course, either by not coming back or by disturbing the learning of all involved. The teacher must design for the inclusion of all.

All teams, like all organizations, are limit situations. This is a useful term Freire (1972) uses to describe a human situation that has its limits. The limit situation is always a given. We do not work in a perfect world. Our task is not to make a perfect team but to perfect ourselves in the effort to make our team work effectively.

This philosophical approach assumes that perfect systems are not the end of learning. The end of learning is the personal development of the learner. Using dialogue, we can use every limit situation as a learning opportunity.

In a team, learning is enhanced by peers. We know that peers hold significant authority with adults, more authority than most teachers. Peers often have similar experience. They can challenge one another in ways a teacher cannot. Peers create safety for the learner who is struggling with complex concepts and skills or attitudes. I have seen significant mentoring go on in teams: peers helping one another, often with surprising clarity, tenderness, and skill.

Teams invite the welcome energy of competition. If we look at this word *com* + *petition*, we can see opportunity: *com* = with; *petition* = asking. We are asking together. There can, of course, be destructive competition among teams in a win/lose situation. Constructive competition is structured so that teams work together in the learning process—and have fun together—manifesting their learning with a certain pride in their achievement as a team.

Teams present new problems in the learning situation, however, as people must *learn* how to work together efficiently. We need time at the beginning of a course to invite learners to examine their roles in the team. There are group maintenance roles and task maintenance roles. As a team considers how these roles are being acted out, they can use praxis to examine how their team can work more efficiently. When learning tasks are deeply related to themes and time is adequate for the task, adult learners will work energetically in teams.

Accountability of individual learners to their own objectives, and to their teams, can be problematic. When, in rare cases, a learner shows indifference or reluctance to join in a task, it is the teacher's responsibility to step in and work with that person. Perhaps the person should not be in the learning session at all. This is a decision to be made by both the adult learner and the teacher. The principle of safety is operative here. And that involves respect for the individual, for the teacher, and for the entire group. The challenging story of team development in Zimbabwe (Chapter Twelve) is unusual. Prior to the literacy training program, these young men and women had been members of military units in the guerrilla army that fought for Zimbabwe's independence. Now they were learning to be literacy coordinators with an entirely new idea of teamwork.

Principle 11: Engagement

In Chapter Thirteen we see how a hospice team's engagement in the learning and in the action plans that followed was a vital principle to assure the quality of their learning. Through our learning tasks we invite learners to put themselves into the learning task—to jump, so to speak, into the deep water. When learners are deeply engaged, working in small groups or teams, it is often difficult to extricate them from the delight of that learning.

Principle 12: Accountability

Accountability is one of the foremost principles of adult learning. The design of learning events must be accountable to the learners. What was proposed to be taught must be taught; what was meant to be learned must be learned; the skills intended to be gained must be manifest in all the learners; the attitudes taught must be manifest; the knowledge conveyed must be visible in adult learners' language and reasoning. Accountability is a synthesis principle—the result of using all the other principles as well as the beginning of the action.

Chapter Fourteen is about a training event with doctors in Bangladesh. It offers a surprising example of the need for accountability. This story relates also to the issue of role. The doctors in the training program had a very hard time accepting that they needed to learn how to teach. Their role in their own country is such that they receive little personal or professional feedback. As they learned the principles and practiced them among themselves, they found their role changing.

Ancient hierarchical relationships do not lend themselves to dialogue. They are reminiscent of the hierarchical system of the medieval church and state that we inherited and shaped into systems in industry, school, university, and government. That historic relationship can be changed only on a small scale, one event at a time. We must be aware of what occurs, however, when the hierarchical relationship is *not* changed. Dialogue is defeated; adult learning is impeded.

Thomas Kuhn offers us a useful hypothesis: change of a pattern (he calls it a paradigm shift) will only occur when the present pattern has proven itself ineffective and impossible to live with (Kuhn, 1970). Part of my job in this book is to contrast patterns, demonstrating how inefficient the hierarchical pattern is when we are attempting to teach adults. If we are not sensitive to the cultural perspectives and value systems of the people we teach, though, we will not succeed in designing and effecting a dialogue with them.

As we work in our complex global and national society to reach adults who need knowledge, skills, and new, healthier attitudes to build healthy lives, we can design for dialogue, which has been proven to work in helping adults learn. The basic assumption is that all learners come with both experience and personal perceptions of the world based on that experience, and all deserve respect. Popular education, nonformal adult learning, community education, and training are most effective when we honor that assumption. In the twelve chapters of Part Two we will hear stories of adult learning situations based on it.

2

How the Principles Inform Course Design and Teaching

This chapter contains two examples that show how the twelve principles inform the design and teaching of a group of adult learners. The principles work equally well in both cases, although the setting, the participants, and the purpose of the course are different for each.

In the first example, we have been invited by a small not-for-profit organization to design and teach its staff and board members how to have effective meetings. They live from meeting to meeting in this organization, and find many of their meetings to be time-wasting formalities.

The Seven Steps: How to Hold Good Meetings

Our use of the simple Seven Steps of Planning—Who, Why, When, Where, What For, What, and How—honors the fact that we begin with the learners as subjects of this learning process. The seven steps focus the design and invite consideration and use of the principles as we make our plan. They are integral for us in the design of adult learning as dialogue.

The first question to be answered is Who: Who are these learners? We want to know them as subjects of this learning and, moreover, to learn through the needs assessment all we can of their cultural perspective and what they consider the immediate needs for learning about the topic. The organization is ten years old, has a board of seven men and women from prestigious community agencies, and wants to learn these skills to assure comprehensive participation in every aspect of their operation. "Who needs what as defined by whom" is the question at the heart of the needs assessment.

The next planning question is Why: What is the problem that calls for this course? We see that the agency is ten years old and needs information and skills about how to make its meetings work. Board meetings are often tense and stiff. The board is missing the verve and spontaneity that exist among the staff. The director needs a process and a set of guidelines for the many kinds of meetings she designs and runs—with the board, with clients, with the community, with fundraisers.

As we examine the Who and Why questions, we use virtually all of the principles: the staff and board members themselves will be the decision makers of this course, the content must have immediate usefulness to them, their cultural perspectives are diverse and must all be honored, the roles among the group will have to be clarified and respected, safety will be assured with adequate time together and a careful sequencing of tasks for the learners to do in small groups, as part of a larger team. They will have reinforcement of what they are learning about designing and facilitating effective meetings as they use new skills in the course of the training session.

Two other logistical questions also invite us to honor these learners as decision makers or subjects of their own learning: When and Where. It is vital to choose a time that is convenient for this unique group. The staff could come on a weekday, as part of their work, but the board members cannot. So the decision is a delicate one. The timing of a community education event is virtually always a political decision. How can we decide on a time that honors the safety of all? We finally have the board and staff decide on a time when the greatest number can be present. The planning question "When" invites serious consideration of just how much can be taught in the available time. In this case, the staff and board agree to a two-hour session. We set achievement-based objectives and content appropriate to that time frame.

Where such an event occurs is another decision that involves many of the principles. We need an environment that feels safe for all and has room for small-group work at tables. It also must be conveniently close to all the participants, many of whom do not have access to automobiles. These considerations involve a synthesis of virtually all the principles, honoring the life situation of all the learners. The director polls the group and decides to hold the sessions in a church lounge near the office. People can get to it by foot and it is close to their homes.

What For is the question we use to set achievement-based objectives. That is, we are mutually accountable to achieve the objectives before the end of the course. All the responses to What For are verbs, so we honor the fact that learners must do something (psychomotor activity) with what they are learning if they are to know that they know when the course is over. We offer the director a draft set of objectives based on our needs assessment. It is her role to edit them and assure us as designers and teachers that we are on the right track. We answer the question What For and set the achievement-based objectives for this course; by the end of this two-hour workshop we all will have:

1. Named some problems we have with meetings
2. Examined a list of guidelines for a good meeting
3. Added to that list
4. Named the guidelines that are most useful to us
5. Practiced using at least one guideline
6. Distinguished between a consultative and a deliberative voice

Such achievement-based objectives assure accountability and honor the learners as subjects—decision makers—of their own learning. Each objective will be related to a learning task that will involve cognitive, affective, and psychomotor activities and content. The sequence of the objectives is related to the sequence in those tasks, and each reinforces the previous learning.

The question that invites the content of a course is What. In formal education, the professor usually begins planning with What: the skills, attitudes, and knowledge that will be imparted to the learners. In this approach to learning, using these principles, the adults' needs, discovered during the needs assessment, sort out the What. Guidelines for the design and facilitation of a good meeting are classic and clearly set out in current literature. How those guidelines are interpreted and then organized, however, must be determined by the context. We finally decided, in conference with the director, that this group wanted to examine a comprehensive list of preparatory steps for designing an effective meeting, as well as questions about the process of the meeting.

The principles of immediacy and accountability oblige us to take the raw content of concepts, skills, and attitudes and weave it into a useful set for this particular group. The principle of praxis enables us to shape our plan so that members will do what they are learning and then examine what they are doing, in teams, as subjects, decision makers, from their own cultural perspective. Such an approach frees the teacher to listen and to design, to set learning tasks that are accountable for achieving the set objectives, to teach the content knowing there is no cultural intrusion, since she is not the only decision maker. She will be able to respond using the language of the learners as they do the learning tasks. Adult learners know when they are being respected. The rise in energy and creativity is manifest in the group of learners when they discover how the design honestly invites their opinion and respects their life experience. The content we decided to teach relates directly to the achievement-based objectives. This is an iterative process: What For is represented by verbs; What is represented by nouns that are in some ways a repetition of the objectives. The content (What) of this two-day workshop includes classic problems that arise at meetings of nonprofit organizations, sixteen guidelines for an effective meeting, and the distinction between consultative and deliberative voices in a meeting. Objectives 2, 3, 4, and 5 invite work with the guidelines; one of the guidelines speaks of the distinction between a consultative voice (suggestion) and a deliberative voice (decision).

The How is the action program—a set of sequenced learning tasks through which the staff and their board will, in teams, use the concepts they are learning to design and practice having an effective meeting. Learning tasks are open questions put to a small group for response using the resources supplied by the teacher. In this case, each learning task had a worksheet of materials. As small groups completed the tasks, they shared their responses and we collated them. An effective meeting emerged, step by step, as each new step reinforced the learning and decisions in the previous one.

What is the teacher's role while learners are doing their learning tasks? We are resources for the process and for the content. We invite questions and respond to them without giving a lengthy dissertation on the issue. Our central job is to prepare the design through our comprehensive use of the Seven Steps of Planning and to set tasks in careful sequence. Once the learning starts, through the immediate praxis of the small groups, we get out of the way but stay available, as resources, for questions on process or content.

It is our task to collate and organize the responses of the groups when their tasks are completed. During this collation there is often occasion for editorial comment: linking one point with another, showing significant differences in points of view, sharing related experiences from similar groups. While learners enjoy this commentary, teachers must realize that this is not the only learning time. Students have learned through the doing. If our commentary, coming from another cultural perspective, does not seem reasonable to them, they will object to it or switch it off. Their objections are a vital part of the dialogue, clarifying both the materials and the tasks.

The next section outlines the tasks we set for this program and

the materials we shared with students, including the critical incident, a problem-based case study. Note that the case study is set out
as a problem in order to evoke the affective response of the group,
and to bring that to bear in their learning. Paulo Freire (1970)
speaks of "problem-posing education," which means that our design
task is to pose an immediate problem and give the small groups
some resources they need to resolve it. In that resolution is the
learning.

A Sample Design

This is a sample of a two-hour workshop, using the Seven Steps of
Planning and all the principles and practices we have been reviewing. It is called "We've Got to Stop Meeting Like This!"

Who: Eighteen staff and board members of a ten-year-old
nonprofit group.

Why: They need to make their many meetings more efficient.

When: Thursday evening for two hours, from 7–9 pm.

What: Classic problems that arise at meetings of nonprofit
organizations, sixteen guidelines for an effective meeting,
and the distinction between consultative and deliberative
voices in a meeting.

Where: St. Paul's church library; six tables of threes.

What For: By the end of this two-hour workshop, we will
have named some problems we have at meetings, examined
a list of guidelines for an effective meeting, and made the
distinction between deliberative and consultative voices in
a meeting.

How: Four learning tasks using these materials: a case study
and a set of sixteen guidelines for effective meetings. Task 4
is an evaluation task.

Learning Tasks

Task 1:   Read this story about a troubled meeting in Chicago. At your table express your response to it.

Task 2:   Read the set of guidelines for the preparation, facilitation, and recording of a meeting. Using these guidelines, decide at your table what would have made the meeting more effective. (We'll share a sample of your responses.)

Task 3:   Which items in this set are most important for your meetings? Which would not apply at all to meetings where you work? What would you add to this list? (We will share all that you offer.)

Task 4:   How do you know you know? If you were teaching a group how to have an effective meeting, what would you include from this checklist?

Case Study: A Troubled Meeting

Here is a typical situation in a busy not-for-profit agency in Chicago. A critical meeting has been called for 4 PM by the agency director. He announced this meeting at the 11 AM coffee break that morning. It is Friday, December 19.

There is an agenda that the director has prepared. It has twelve items on it. When people arrive at 4 PM, somewhat reluctantly, they discover that the director is not present. He was called to a critical meeting by his boss upstairs.

The meeting finally begins at 4:20 when the director arrives, a bit breathless from running. He does not have the materials he needs to distribute to staff for Item 1 on his agenda.

A resource person has been invited to discuss budget problems with the staff. This budget specialist has not been briefed adequately. She does not understand that decisions on budget are made not by the staff but by the director and the board.

The writing on the blackboard is hardly legible because the

room is dark on this wintry Friday afternoon. No one has been designated recorder of the meeting, so when the blackboard is erased, the many points recorded there are lost.

The meeting ends abruptly when the director is called out for an important phone call from the Kellogg Foundation about a proposal due to them on Monday. There is no indication when this group will meet again. People go home quite dispirited.

A Set of Guidelines

Preparation

1. Has an agenda been prepared for the meeting?
2. Has this agenda been shared beforehand with all who are to be involved in the meeting? How long beforehand?
3. Is this meeting really necessary, or could the information be shared in another, less expensive way?
4. Have the resource people been fully informed about the participants, the purpose of the meeting, their slot time, and their expected purpose in the meeting?
5. Does everyone have minutes of the last meeting so that there is continuity?
6. Have all the materials for the meeting been gathered: documents, audiovisual support, and so forth?

The Meeting Itself

7. Is it clear who the chairperson or facilitator of the meeting is?
8. Is time sufficient for all tasks on the agenda?
9. Does everyone present have all the necessary materials for the meeting?
10. Are people clear about the difference between a consultative voice (a suggestion) and a deliberative voice (a decision)?

11. Has a recorder or secretary been appointed to keep a record of the meeting?

12. What about the meeting room? Lights? Space? Table room? Blackboard or easel and flipchart? Audiovisual apparatus?

13. Does the facilitator/chair know how to move briskly from agenda item to agenda item?

14. How does the group deal with an obtrusive member? A pair of obtrusive members? (Obtrusive means not cooperating with the process of the meeting.)

15. Are all the participants feeling good about their opportunity to speak during the meeting—that is, is the meeting fully open?

16. How are questions for clarification asked? How about substantive questions on the issue? Do people see the difference?

Evaluation

The final learning task is an evaluation task. We evaluate the immediate usefulness of a learning event, often by using two open questions that form a force-field analysis: What was most useful to you in this program? What would you suggest we change? This approach assumes there are positive and negative fields in any event, and as we name and analyze the forces within each field we can enhance the next event. Such a task assumes that learners are subjects, that they have been engaged, and that they now are accountable for responding in terms of the objectives we have set together. Their cultural perspective is invited by such a task.

Long-range evaluation occurs some time after the event. This process invites examination of indicators demonstrating how learners are using the skills, knowledge, and attitudes learned in the course. In this case, we gave the group a set of questions and invited the director to call a meeting to respond to those questions three months from this date. Some of the longitudinal evaluation questions were: How has the set of guidelines for having an effective meeting affected your work? How have your customary meetings changed? Which guidelines were used most frequently?

In the next example, we see the preparation and design of a training program for National Service (NS) staff who are about to teach young recruits how to work in small rural communities. We begin with the Seven Steps of Planning.

The Seven Steps: National Service Training

- Who: There are sixteen men and women in this course. All are recent graduates of small colleges, and most have majored in sociology, community development, or psychology. None of them has done any graduate work or had long-term employment. They are therefore ripe for learning a new way of teaching, and for the shock of this approach, which will demand that they do what they are learning before they dare to teach it. Why sixteen of them? This design will be a model for future training, and therefore the numbers are restricted to maintain quality—and we know how scale affects a learning situation. The course members will be working with similar groups of sixteen in future NS staff training programs.

- Why: The situation that calls for this training course is obvious: these graduates will soon be teaching hundreds of young National Service staff members how to work productively with small rural communities. Since the participants have just come from a formal university setting, it is vital that they learn a new way of teaching to use with the NS staff. They need to be certain not only of the content of their curriculum of training but also of the quality of the process.

- When: This is a two-week program, allowing for some class work and then intensive fieldwork in a small rural community in Missouri.

- Where: The training takes place at a community training center in rural Missouri, near a small agricultural town.

- What For: These are the achievement-based objectives set up for the two-week training program. All sixteen participants will *do* what is set out here, and having done it, will know they know how to do it. Note how different these are from traditional behavioral objectives, which state: They will be able to. . . . Here we say: By the end of the two weeks, all sixteen participants will have:

  - Examined theories of adult learning
  - Distinguished between monologue and dialogue
  - Examined communication theories
  - Practiced doing a community needs assessment
  - Examined the principles and practices of popular education as they are modeled in this course
  - Practiced designing training programs for NS staff using the Seven Steps of Planning and all the principles and practices of popular education
  - Read and reviewed a selected set of books and articles on community education and popular education: Freire, Vella, and so on
  - Practiced specific communication skills in the field
  - Set criteria for communication between NS staff and the community
  - Practiced active listening in the community
  - Completed the record forms for the government office
  - Designed a two-week training course for NS staff, using the same content and process

These objectives will be achieved through the set of learning tasks in our design. The participants will *know that they know* because they have just done what they were learning.

- What: Content includes theories of adult learning; monologue and dialogue; community needs assessment; the Seven Steps of Planning; communication skills; listening skills; the principles and practices of popular education; how to complete record forms for the government.

- How: The topical program, learning tasks and materials, will be presented to the sixteen participants before they come to the course, along with the objectives. This is to provide them with *safety*, which we have learned is a vital principle of adult learning. Such safety has been proven to invite honesty and spontaneity in the dialogue, to evoke real feelings, and to enable learners to take off their masks right up front. When these individuals are working with the community, they will have to be honest—to be themselves, their best selves. They can begin that right on day one of this course.

Here is a sample of the learning tasks they will perform to achieve a few of the objectives. The first objective examined, theories of adult learning, leads to this learning task: In small groups of threes, describe the best learning experience in your life. Analyze that experience. What were the factors that made you learn? After we review your factors, we will compare them with this set of factors named by Malcolm Knowles and his associates when doing research on adult learning. They discovered that adults learn (1) when they feel themselves respected, (2) when the new learning is related to their life experience, and (3) when the new learning has some immediate usefulness to them; moreover, they learn (4) 20 percent of what they hear, 40 percent of what they hear and see, and 80 percent of what they do or discover for themselves. As the sixteen participants assess their own learning, analyze it, and then compare their factors with those named by adult education specialists, they come to trust their own experience and to feel self-respect. Most of the time, adults will have named all the factors discovered by the researchers in Knowles's work. A final open question invites them to apply their discoveries to both the training they will do with NS staff and their work in the community: "How can this help you in your work in the community and with the new staff?"

The small groups provide safety, as adults can speak more openly with three or four of their peers. The informal design of the room, with tables of threes or fours, breaks down the stereotype of the classroom with an all-knowing teacher and passive learners. The small groups quickly become learning *teams*, working together to help one another reflect and learn, building a spirit of constructive competitiveness in the room.

Before the students come to the course, I will speak with at least eight of the sixteen, sharing the objectives, asking them what their needs are in relation to the new job they are starting. I expect to hear that they want to learn how to teach the new NS staff effectively, and to practice meeting the community and working with them themselves. They will undoubtedly express concern about the paperwork, since federal government reporting systems are notoriously complex. Many will say they want a sure sense of what the goals and objectives of the National Service program are. This *needs assessment* helps us determine which objectives will take priority. Our doing a needs assessment with them may ensure that they will do such a needs assessment with the community. We know we are modeling a new way of teaching at every step.

The objective of completing the record forms for the government office leads to this learning task: Read this case study of a set of community events led by National Service staff. At your tables, complete the record sheet to reflect all the work done that week. Directions for filling out the form are there for you. Use us as resources to answer any of your questions. Share your completed forms with one other table after ten minutes. What are your questions?

This learning task invites all participants to act as *subjects*, decision makers of their own learning, to work as a team and to teach one another, to monitor one another and to suggest changes. The *role of the professor* has changed dramatically here. Our job is to design the case study and set the tasks, sit still, pay attention, and be available as a resource when they have questions. We will review each table's form and help students with parts that are obscure or ambiguous. Honoring and respecting adults as subjects of their own learning uncovers endless sources of energy for cooperation. We have often found that suggestions from the learners about such a technical task are innovative and creative and can make the task less difficult for all involved. The professor is learning too.

Later learning tasks will take the NS trainers into the community and invite them to assess and analyze their involvement. *Sequence and reinforcement* are at work in our setting such tasks after we have done serious work on basic learning and communication theory. We realize that our effort is never to test; it is always to teach. When adults have adequate reinforcement of a skill, knowledge, or attitude and are invited to use it after adequate initial work with it, they usually can do it well. It is the instructor's job to know the moment to invite autonomous action of the learner.

In this National Service training course we have insisted on sixteen participants so that we can get to know each one and can establish a sound relationship for learning. During the two-week course, the instructor is a resource, an advocate, a counselor. In an adult learning situation like this, the formal distance between professor and student that one recalls from school days is not helpful. If we want the learning dialogue to occur, we must establish an environment for dialogue.

The group will have learned that *respect* is the most important variable in adult learning, and learners will then go out to the community for an initial set of meetings. As they try to show respect for the midwestern farmers they meet at the PTA, the Grange meetings, the county extension seminars, they have the tools for *praxis*, for analyzing their encounters. Each time they go out, their efforts are more professional, more effective. People feel they are being listened to, being heard. That word gets around town very fast indeed.

Because of the respect they themselves will have encountered in the training course, they will consciously respect the community members they meet. We will have been very explicit about the cross-cultural situation here, asking in the training course: How do you spell *respect* in rural Missouri? The staff will have read and studied a great deal about this modern agricultural society and its current problems. They will have spent time at the open market, the shopping mall in town, the library, the city hall, and various organizational meetings, introducing themselves and talking with citizens. This learning task involves *ideas, actions, and feelings.* As adult learners, the participants need all three to know that they know enough about the community to seriously plan projects with its members. Our students will teach the National Service staff they train in the same way, aware that adult learning always involves more than cognitive content—it involves affective and psychomotor activities as well. Ideas, feelings, and actions—all work together to invite the adult NS staff to learn about the real world they will be serving.

Throughout the training course, the men and women are fully engaged in learning tasks in their teams in the classroom and in the community. Their *engagement* is ensured by the immediacy of the learning task, which relates to the immediacy of the course objective that the task is implementing. Without this engagement, learners simply cannot learn. Our job is to design effective achievement-based objectives—and corresponding learning tasks and materials. When we do this well, we are in fact accountable to the NS staff and can assure them that they will learn what we have set out for them to learn. They will know they know at the end of the two-week period. Such accountability is never accidental. It is ensured by design.

Since this training course is in fact a training of trainers, and the sixteen participants will be teaching what they have just learned to new NS staff members, the success of the course will be immediately manifest. The participants will design a training program to use with new staff and then lead parts of their program in teams of two. We will videotape their microteaching and offer them feedback on both the design and their teaching skills.

In the next twelve chapters, you will read stories showing how the twelve principles of adult learning demonstrated through the two examples in this chapter—engagement; respect; safety; teamwork; sound relationship; action, ideas, and feelings; accountability; needs assessment; immediacy; role of the professor; sequence and reinforcement; and praxis—were significant in the design and teaching of a particular course for a particular group of people. My experience and reflection have convinced me that these principles, given a fair chance, will work with adults anywhere.

PART TWO

The Principles
in Action—
Across Cultures
and Around the World

3

Needs Assessment: The First Step in Dialogue

How do you set learning objectives in a strange land, in a strange language, for a strange and unprecedented relief and development activity? How do you teach a group of young Ethiopians and an Afar nomad woman to responsibly implement a relief program? How do you do this under intense time pressure, with over half a million lives depending on the knowledge and skills of the young staff? Who are the natural definers of these learning objectives? The teacher? The program directors? The learners themselves? The government officials? How do you select, from all the conflicting objectives, those that can be achieved in the available time? How do you assure accountability and quality in the performance of the young staff?

The Problem and the Setting

On October 23, 1984, Tom Brokaw of NBC news shocked millions of Americans at their dinner tables by presenting a raw picture of the drought in northern Ethiopia. Before the evening news program was over, telephones were ringing at Save the Children offices in Westport, Connecticut, with offers of financial support from sympathetic men and women all over the country. They had rarely been so touched and so moved to offer whatever they could to stop the horrific hunger they had witnessed on that ninety-second TV clip. The agency had no program at that time in Ethiopia. It was their British colleagues in the TV film that touched the hearts of people around the world. As funds for Ethiopia flooded in, decisions were made to set up a program as quickly as possible.

By early December, the government of Ethiopia had named an area in which to focus efforts at relief and development. It was Yfrat and Timuga, a district with one town called Epheson, seven hours north of Addis Ababa. A medical doctor and a manager were in Addis setting up the program with the Ethiopian government as international groups coordinated the relief services. The staff of the new program were to be hired in the area and trained there before starting work. As director of training, I was sent to Ethiopia to design and lead their training. I was responsible to the director of the Ethiopian program to get the staff into action as soon as possible, with all the skills and knowledge they would need to manage a million-dollar operation.

I knew nothing about Ethiopia and little about the drought that I had not read in the daily papers. How could I prepare myself to teach the Ethiopian people who might be hired for this program? Further, I had no idea what skills and knowledge I would be teaching, since it was still not clear what the program was going to look like. Both the director of primary health and the Ethiopian program director were determined not to open yet another relief station where mothers brought starving babies in to die before dying themselves. What was the alternative?

Resources were abundant, thanks to the generosity of Americans touched by the horrors of the drought. How could we use these resources wisely and teach Ethiopian staff to do the same? How could we make these resources stretch beyond the relief effort into a brighter, drought-free development phase? The doctor had a plan. He intended, drawing on his long experience in Zaire and Haiti, to put into place a relief program that would bring food to the villagers in their homes in the mountains while laying the groundwork for a local health system that could grow into the future.

In Addis Ababa, however, where we both were staying, he was

working fourteen-hour days establishing credibility with Ethiopian government staff, channeling medical and relief supplies that were flooding the airport of Addis Ababa to the project area, meeting leaders from Yfrat and Timuga. I needed to hear his plan, amorphous as it still was, in order to begin a training design. I could not even find time to have a meal with him, much less a briefing on the overall plan.

Wisely, I made no training design until I could find that time. I did no planning because I was not yet a definer of learning objectives. Until we had a clear conceptual framework for the skills, knowledge, and attitudes the staff needed to learn in order to do the job, I could not set up a program. As a wise man once said: "Don't just do something, sit there." I sat there. It was a great temptation to get started—to design a plan for training in the familiar modes of the agency's development programs. It was not easy to sit there, to study Ethiopian history and read the literature to get some sense of the culture and the painful problem, to talk to old friends from Tanzania I found working in Addis Ababa. All around me swirled a frenzy of activity. I sat still, reading, observing, visiting, listening, waiting for time with the decision makers.

One Sunday afternoon the promised time arrived. I locked the door of our hotel room, sat down the good doctor, and said: "Talk!" My questions followed a familiar pattern. We used the Seven Steps of Planning to get a comprehensive framework of the plan.

Who were the new staff to be? All of the adult population of Yfrat and Timuga who could move to Addis had done so. Those who remained had been decimated by the drought. The only available staff were youth from the towns along the main road that had a food supply line from Addis Ababa. These young people would be recent high school graduates with no English and no prospect of jobs except this one. They had no work experience. They had no health-related skills. They felt themselves, as townsfolk, a class above the peasant population they would be serving. They would be strangers to the mountain villages where they would be working.

The situation (Why) was the drought, of course, which called for relief operations at intense levels. What about the overall plan? How could I come to understand the doctor's vision clearly enough to share it with the youth? They had to be made to see that this was not merely a relief operation but a process toward ongoing development systems.

The objectives of the relief and development program were, first, to get food to the people so that they did not have to leave their homes. Then we were to establish systems for agriculture, health, and transportation from those villages—systems that could lead to social and political strength in the near future. Drought was not a stranger to these folks. They needed their local systems strengthened so that they could handle both drought and ample harvests. The training would have to make this clear. What would we teach in the short time available? This, in fact, was what had to be determined soon.

The Learners

It was a cold afternoon in Epheson. The chairman of the village stood and interviewed the gathered group of sixteen young men and women. The girls were shy and quiet, the boys clearly desperate for the job. (Since we had no other source of supply for our staff, their concern was unnecessary.) But they knew no English! How in the world could we create a dialogue with them? How could I teach them what they needed to know to do the job? Into the midst of this shy and gangly group of young people strode the answer to my fearful questions: Fatuma, a mature, lean Afar nomad, a leader of her tribe. She had asked the chairman if she could join the group in training so that she could assure her people that they too would be part of the relief and development program. The Afar lived in tents in the mountains herding camels. They and their herds were dying of the drought and needed this program desperately.

The chairman looked questioningly at us. Would I accept Fatuma into the group? She could not speak Amharic or English. She was old enough to be the mother of the young men and women standing around waiting to be hired. She stood there, tall and sure, with her rifle on her shoulder, smiling hopefully at me and at the men who would make this life-and-death decision. "I want her!" I smiled back at Fatuma and began a profound but wordless friendship. I speak no Afar. Fatuma speaks no English. But we have communicated deeply in all the years since that day in December 1984. I knew intuitively that Fatuma, without words, could define learning needs for the group and for me.

Months later, after the training, when I was leaving Ethiopia, Fatuma made a short speech in her native Afar tongue. It was translated for me into English: "When these troubles are over, I will invite you to our Afar camp in the mountains. I will kill a camel to celebrate your coming, and the young men and women of our tribe will dance for you!" We had begun a friendship on that cold December afternoon, a friendship that would lead to learning on all sides. Here is the key to adult learning. Without it there is no honest defining of learning needs, no dialogue, no listening: the key is the loving, respectful relationship of learner and teacher. As we see in this instance, such a relationship does not even need a common language.

The Program and the Process

The sixteen young men and women went home for their gear and settled into the Epheson hotel with Fatuma and me. The hotel ($1 a night and highly overpriced) provided a large room for the training. Nobody suspected that we did not yet have a training course. We had hired an Ethiopian civil servant from Addis Ababa to be translator. He knew English and some Afar. He was to work by my side for the three weeks of "training." The rest of the team was going back to Addis to continue organizing logistics for the start of the program in four weeks' time. I still did not know what they wanted these young people to know. Once again, I locked the doctor in our hotel room and threatened, begged, cajoled: "Look, you are the *definer* of the skills, knowledge, and attitudes these people need to run this program. You have to let me in on the big picture."

Dr. Warren Berggren described his vision: in lieu of building a relief station, we hoped to build a transport system that could bring food to the abandoned villages, trusting that people would return home when they discovered there was food available at home. Mountain villagers in Ethiopia have an incredible "bamboo wireless" that did indeed get this information to families as far away as Addis Ababa. Then they could nurse their children back to health, feeding them amply from the relief stores, plant when the rains came, and harvest in the new season. They could continue with their lives in their familiar places. The agency would provide development services: health systems, seeds, agricultural education, water systems, all that could get them started again on a sound basis. The government would then take over these services as basic social infrastructure for this area.

These villages near Epheson in the mountains of Yfrat and Timuga were remote and virtually inaccessible. Rough roads could be built. Indeed, they were completed by the very men who came back home to find food. The sixteen young staff people would be expected to organize the villagers to receive food, distribute food, vaccinate the infants, give vitamin A to prevent blindness among infants, measure and weigh all children and document the information so that those at greatest risk could receive special care, enroll all families so that continued services could be assured, identify the very sick and dying for emergency care, give that emergency care at an aid station, explain the long-range program to mothers so they would bring the children for continued care and vaccinations. There we had it. At last the learning needs—the skills, knowledge, and attitudes these young people needed to do the job—had been defined by the program's directors. I gulped and then asked: "What else do they need to learn in four weeks?"

Dr. Berggren and I drew great charts of protocols as they would work themselves out in the villages. A protocol, in this situation, was a system of related activities, in a very strict sequence, that got a job done with assured quality. These protocols related one to the other so that the whole program could be seen as a flow of activities. Dr. Berggren's definition of learning needs was straightforward and comprehensive: this was it! I could have at that moment turned his protocol into activities involving specific skills, knowledge, and attitudes and set up a program. The needs assessment, however, was not yet complete. What about the other *definers*? The program director would live with this program long after Dr. Berggren and I had left. What did he want? The political leaders had to know themselves to be in charge of what went on in their region. What did they want? How did these men define the learning needs of the group? What did Fatuma and the young men and women want from this training course and in the program? My job was to fit all these needs together while honoring my own definition of learning needs.

One thing we decided early: all sixteen of the youth and Fatuma would know how to do all the tasks in the protocol. There would be no specialists on this small staff. I asked the program director to spend time with the political leaders, describing the protocols and the overall program, asking them their hopes for the training. He and I had some time together, but later developments would show it was not nearly enough for me to know his intentions. Perhaps we should have designed a system for continued input from his office on the training event. He, after all, was their supervisor and would be responsible for the success of their work and that of the overall program. Here was a case where role clarification was inadequate. And we were to suffer the consequences of this error.

We later recognized that in our haste we had left a crucial element out of this picture as definers of learning needs for this training: the parents themselves and the men and women of Yfrat and Timuga who would be served by this group of town youth. A challenging strategic question is: How could I have gotten their opinion on this design?

Who Needs What as Defined by Whom?

This useful question, from Dr. Thomas Hutchinson of the University of Massachusetts School of Education, Amherst, proved a useful instrument in discovering the learning needs of the group. I discovered that such a question is never definitively answered. It must be asked again and again. New situations, new complexities, arise to change the Who and the What and even the definers, the Whom.

Who would teach this course? I might design it, but I surely could not teach them to give vaccinations or do emergency aid. We could get the local government doctor in Epheson to do that. I could teach most of the other items on the protocol with the help of our translator and, as it proved, my friend Fatuma. We started on a Monday morning in December. The young people were anxious to make good since this was the only job in town. The translator was apprehensive. Fatuma sat proudly at a table by herself. I felt very much alone in the mountains of northern Ethiopia, immensely frightened by the prospect ahead of me. These young people and Fatuma had to be ready to begin the relief program when the program director arrived with the first shipments of relief food early in January. Over four hundred thousand men, women, and children waited upon the success of this program. Their lives depended on it. This was an educational challenge to match all others.

As a diagnostic task I invited them to draw a map of the area, putting in all the vital information they thought I should know. I learned that they did know a great deal about the people of Epheson (the town) and less about those in the mountain villages. Fatuma, of course, knew her people well. I learned that we had two artists in the group. I watched them all work together and saw that the boys took over from the girls, yet were quick to defer to Fatuma. I watched who made decisions about what information should go on the rough map. This was all done in Amharic and Afar, words translated into English here and there, with much laughter and complete anarchy in the design of the large wall map that emerged. We used that map throughout the course, adjusting it to reality as we learned more.

The dialogue had begun. The initial problem was my education, not theirs. This was a shock to them, I could see. This was not like any school they had ever been to before. I asked each person to cite the most important item on the map. As their replies were translated, and I documented them, I learned a bit about each person's value system. I could see that this needs assessment was going to be an ongoing process. From among the natural friends who had been visible in the drawing of the map, we set up learning teams for accountability. The teams were mixed: men and women. Two of the young men knew some Afar, as I had noticed, so they were able to work in a team with Fatuma. Nothing would be so useful in this training program as their working in teams: preparing them to work in teams in the field, making it safe for them to make mistakes, to question, to be unsure, and creating a quality control group of peers. Competition among these teams was soon evident—not a destructive competition but a natural *com* + *petition*, asking together how the job could be done well, done better. Lavish affirmation, a central factor in this approach to adult learning, was soon working, even through translation, to get these young people and Fatuma to relax into the job. I discovered that these sixteen youth were literate and numerate, knew Ethiopian history, and felt deeply about the drought and the need for their country to become self-reliant. They understood that the ravaging of trees from the mountains to provide firewood and charcoal for the growing urban population had caused this drought. They evidenced little knowledge of the sociopolitical forces involved in this geophysical catastrophe. Since they were semiurban youth from towns along a main road, they had much to learn from rural Ethiopians. The culture of the roadside is not the culture of the mountainside, as they were soon to discover.

Imagine what would have happened if I had asked this group directly, through the translator, what they thought they needed to learn. Such an approach to needs assessment would have resulted in nothing authentic or useful. The design of the map, the open questions, the dialogue among the participants, all were spontaneous and natural. Even if I could not understand the words, I knew they were naming real needs, vital issues, important factors in this complex program. They felt *safe* in the learning environment. I had prepared large charts of the overall program as we envisioned it, with the protocol steps dramatically indicated via stick figures. After going through the entire scenario, through translation, step by step, I asked them to come up and to write, in teams of twos, the Amharic words that described each step. The charts became a bright mass of Cyrillic characters, and the teams argued loudly over what had been written. Again I was on the outside, looking in, while they defined their job descriptions. They felt safe to disagree with one another. In time, they would feel safe to disagree with me and the program director. I have found that the moment of dissent in a course is a rich moment of learning for all. Modeling a true attitude of inquiry and learning is perhaps the most useful thing a teacher of adults can do.

I had to trust what the translator said. We moved very slowly, of course. I guess I read more of the physical language—the gestures, the questions on foreheads and faces—in this training event than ever I had before. Who needs what as defined by whom? This useful question enabled me to compare their perception of learning needs with the perceptions of other definers I had named. The chairman and other political officers in Epheson had a learning agenda that was not at all surprising: they wanted the group to learn how to use and strengthen the political units in the mountains and to bring the political message of the party to the villagers. I had to accept their agenda. It was up to me to incorporate it into the overall set of objectives of the training. The achievement-based objectives we set were in fact achieved by the end of the three weeks through the learning tasks set up for their training. When senior staff arrived in January, we demonstrated their skills and knowledge by doing all the protocols in sequence on the large field outside the classroom. It was clear they were accountable for all the skills, knowledge, and attitudes taught in the training. How did they know they knew? They did it.

Teamwork

These young people had come from a school system that apparently had never used teamwork in learning. Fatuma, on the other hand, had no trouble working on a team since that was how her Afar people always worked. The small-group work was, as noted earlier, vital in the practice of collaboration and mutual help. Indeed, we had an amusing but significant event during the training. I describe it here to show how leadership within a group emerges if you are in real dialogue with the people involved.

One morning I arrived to start off a series of learning tasks only to discover that the teams had become twos. The love bug had bitten. We now had eight pairs of adolescents looking lovingly at one another, not at all part of their teams nor of the whole project! It was a scene from a high school classroom. What to do? I did not understand this culture, but I knew I needed their attention for the work at hand. I had to address this problem. The translator looked appealingly to me, indicating he had no idea what to do. I had to admit defeat. I stopped the task and stood silently for a moment to catch their eye. Then I said to the translator: "Please tell the group I am going outside. I will be waiting there until they are ready to get to work. If they are not ready to work, I will get into the Land-rover and drive to Addis Ababa where I will call the director and tell them the program cannot continue."

As I walked around outside the hotel, I could feel my legs buckle. Was this culturally appropriate? Would they call my bluff?

How could I call off a million-dollar program, with half a million people's lives at stake, because of a training problem? I thought of the principle of immediacy. These young people were having a severe test of the immediacy of their commitment to this job.

After a very long ten minutes, the translator called me in. There on the front table was Fatuma's rifle. In the room, I found an air of quiet expectancy and rapt attention. I went on setting the task of the day, smiling at Fatuma, who sat innocently in the back row. There was no other evidence of the outbreak of seriousness in the room, but her rifle lay on that front table every day. How she had communicated across cultures, across languages, across generations to those young people is still a mystery. She did it, however, and I learned that I was not the only teacher in that room. The young couples did not bring their heart trouble into their teams any more.

This incident was part of the needs assessment. The young people manifested their need for intimacy; I made my own needs very clear; Fatuma showed her need and capacity for leadership.

Design Challenges

- In any educational program you are designing, how do you discover the learning needs of the participants? How can the WWW question help you: Who needs what as defined by whom? Who are some of the definers of learning needs in your situation?

- What difference would it make to you, as a student in an educational program, to be invited by the professor to share your perception of your own learning needs? How would it make that program more immediate for you if you could do so?

- What are some innovative ways you have used to do a needs assessment?

4

Safety: Creating a Safe Environment for Learning

The principle of safety works for learners and teachers alike in an adult learning situation. There have been many programs of nonformal adult education or community education aimed at development in Third World nations like Tanzania. Many such programs, despite significant investments of funds, personnel, and time, never achieve the goals stated with such assurance in the proposals. What are some the causes of recurrent failure? This story tells of one of those small, failed programs and analyzes the failure. We will examine one community education program and the role of one of the principals, Auni Makame of Musoma near Lake Victoria. We will try to see how the principle of safety, present and absent, made a world of difference in this program.

The Problem and the Setting

Tanzania, listed by the United Nations as one of the twenty-five poorest nations in the world, is engaged in a constant struggle for survival as well as for development. The per capita income still averages a little more than $140 per year. It is estimated that it would take fifty years for a Tanzanian farmer to earn what a poverty-level family earns in one year in the United States. Over 90 percent of the fifteen million people of Tanzania live in the rural areas. Peasant farmers in the rural villages face the formidable tasks of development: building durable homes, constructing latrines, providing a supply of clean water, raising sufficient food for their families, building schools and clinics, raising cash crops to provide some income, building linkage roads to main arteries. Villagers needed education in leadership, education in technical skills for improved agriculture and small enterprise, and education in community organizing.

The Learners

After having studied with Anne Hope and Sally Timmel of the Training for Transformation program in Kenya, my colleague and I designed a proposal for funds for a program we entitled Community Education for Development (CED). We intended to do leadership training using Paulo Freire's problem-posing approach with local Catholic church leaders in the district of Musoma. We were generously funded by a German Catholic development foundation entitled MISEREOR.

Our small education project was an extension arm of the Makoko Family Center in Musoma, which offered a three-week intensive residential course to families in religion, child care, health, homemaking, agriculture, animal husbandry, and politics. Some families returned for Stage II and Stage III of this integrated development course. All returned, after Stage I, to their own village farms with some new ideas after a stimulating new experience. The center had been urged by funding groups to develop an extension program because until CED there had not been any follow-up program or structural support for these families to effect permanent change in their own lives or in their villages. These were the "leaders" we would gather, on site, for continuing training in management, communication, and leadership. Local government leaders were tolerant of the experiment, since it offered the kind of training needed by village leaders. These church folk were often leaders in their community and in the village. We invited local government bureaucrats from the town of Musoma to attend our week-long programs in the neighboring villages and also invited the Catholic church pastors to attend.

Church authorities had given us permission to work in the diocese. They tolerated the idea of two women doing courses for
Makoko families, catechists (local parish teachers of the catechism
or manual of faith), and parish councils on invitation of the local
parish priest. When the learning began to make itself felt in new,
responsible, and accountable attitudes among the villagers however, they quickly began to show new interest.

Mr. Makame, as we called him, had heard of our program in his
village on an island in Lake Victoria. Makame had founded this
village with fishermen who had been coming to fish the lake from
inland villages. When the government ordered all to form *ujamaa*
villages, Makame, himself a fisherman, called together some of his
friends and formed a village on a small island near Musoma. He
later resigned as chairman of the village committee, but the fishermen still thought of him gratefully as their leader. Makame was a
reputed Tanganyika African National Union (TANU) leader who
proved to have good connections within the political party.

Mr. Makame had also started a small industry in Musoma: making chicken feed available to village families. Raising chickens was
a viable household enterprise, but good chicken feed was very hard
to come by. He had a small factory on the outskirts of town where
he made a decent chicken feed out of an incredible assortment of
grains and animal waste. Makame was a local philosopher, an
inventor, a searcher. He had a high school education and was an
avid reader. He made a living through the chicken feed factory for
his wife and three young children, who lived in a small house in
Musoma. So Mr. Makame had the skills to teach what villagers
needed. He had heard of our program from villagers who had done
one of the three-day courses in the village. He liked what he heard
and came to visit us in our little house on the outskirts of the mission. After introducing himself, he said: "I want to come to a
course. I want to learn from you!" Makame felt safe enough to ask
how he could learn from us.

We were honored and delighted. We went to his island village
and led a course with the village committee. He liked what he saw

and told us that TANU in Musoma needed this participative, political, person-centered education in all the villages. He accompanied us for more courses—into villages where Makoko families were the majority, into parish council leadership workshops. It never occurred to me at the time that I was not providing any safety for Mr. Makame or the villagers. They liked him as a man and appreciated his input into the program, enhancing our Swahili, offering stories and images, proverbs and metaphors, from his family history and the political history of the country. But he was a Muslim. And this program was the extension arm of the Makoko Christian Family Center.

The Program and the Process

CED had a Program Committee formed of three parish priests, the priest who directed the Makoko Family Center, and the two of us. The three priests saw CED as a means to train catechists, those who taught newcomers the catechism of the Catholic religion. The Makoko Family Center's director saw CED as a means to follow up the families he had worked with. We, the two women educators on staff, saw the program as broad leadership training, using Freire's problem-posing approach with villagers toward their own personal and community development. As members of this Program Committee we never considered the obvious lack of safety among ourselves, never did any serious reflection on the implications of the process being used, never worked on our own communication problems.

We on the Program Committee needed a CED workshop—in management, leadership, and communication skills—for ourselves. None of the priests on the committee ever attended a CED village course. Only one parish priest who invited us to work with his parish council and catechists ever attended the course. Therefore, these men did not know what we were doing and had never stayed long enough to find out.

Women in the Catholic church had a very specific role at this time: teaching, nursing, cooking, supporting the priests in their efforts. Like faithful wives they were to be backstage, always there when needed, but certainly to be seen and not heard. The two of us in CED did not fit that mold. We did not know enough at the time about the principles of adult learning to provide for ourselves and for all others the safety that would enable all of us to grow together.

The skepticism of the men increased when the Program Committee was presented with our proposal to hire Auni Makame, a Muslim, as an associate in the program. We argued that he would open the program up to many more villages and would be an excellent link to the leadership development efforts of TANU. He would not cost a penny, either, since he could be funded as a Canadian University Services Organization (CUSO) volunteer. This was the first time in history that CUSO had accepted a local Tanzanian as a volunteer. CUSO had also been an early funder of CED and the Makoko Center.

What could we have done at that moment using the principle of safety to redeem this adult learning situation?

- We might have taken a long time to build a relationship between Makame and the bishop and the director and individual priests. Mr. Makame was seen as "the girls' friend."
- We might have organized meetings between the TANU officials and Makame and the church leaders where TANU leaders could speak for themselves about their appreciation of the program.
- We might have organized meetings between Makoko Center families and Makame. He needed only the occasion to build trust with the groups. They would have created the safety we all needed had they had the time to get to know us and Mr. Makame.
- We might have organized opportunities to address parishes at Sunday services about the program. Since our efforts were

planned with individual parish priests, CED did not appear as
a diocesan program. We did not use the institution to make it
safe for them to welcome us. We did not go to each parish
council meeting, or to each church on Sunday morning, or to
the diocesan council. We did not feel safe, as women in an
experimental venture, and we projected that feeling onto the
program.

- We might have taken time in preparation with the Program
  Committee to do strategic planning for CED by asking: Who
  are the stakeholders in this program? What is our collective
  vision? What is our mandate? What actions should we undertake?

The Swahili proverb tells it all: *Kupotea njia ndiko kujua njia!* (By
losing the way one learns the way!) We have learned from this
experience that the safety of the program organizers and teachers
is as important as that of the learners. We now insist that organizations who contract for training make sure that their senior managers take full part in the programs.

Finally, after much negotiation, Makame was accepted. It was
assured that he would not cost the diocese any money and that he
would work under my close direction. Makame had a motorcycle
provided by CUSO for all its volunteers, my colleague and I had
small motorbikes, and together the three of us would roar along the
dirt paths into a sleepy village to wake the residents to a new way of
communicating, managing, and leading. The two of us, American
women, were grateful to have a Tanzanian on board at last, one
who could guide us in ways of teaching more appropriate to rural
village life. Among the three of us there was safety and an exciting
mutual learning dynamic.

Six Considerations

From long experience teaching in Tanzania before this program, I
learned that effective adult learning and teaching is

- *Political*—that is, it has to do with power and the distribution of power both in the process and in the content selected.
- *Problem-posing*—that is, it is a dialogue around adult themes using adult materials evoking affective, psychomotor, and cognitive responses.
- *Part of a whole*—that is, it must have follow-up and continuity and not be a single event raising and then dashing hopes.
- *Participative*—that is, everyone involved will have time to speak, to listen, to be actively engaged in the learning.
- *Person-centered*—that is, its purpose is the development of all the people involved, not merely the covering of the content.
- *Prepared*—that is, from the initial needs assessment through the use of the Seven Steps of Planning, through the design of materials, the learning is designed for this particular group of learners and time is used lavishly to make it ready.

These six considerations served us well, and they served Makame well as he used them in the villages. We had long talks about how they applied in the diverse situations we encountered. At this time we were building a body of theory together as we analyzed the processes and products of the community education program.

A Sample

Despite the serious problems in the program's design, we had some wonderful experiences in villages and parishes. Rural folk were hungry for the chance to tell their stories and share their feelings about local issues. They wanted to know how to be honest leaders among their neighbors, how to manage small projects effectively to bring in needed money and resources, how to communicate better among themselves. There was safety enough in some situations for people to be very honest indeed.

When asked what they most wanted to learn, villagers invariably replied "*kusikilizana.*" This means to hear one another. Most of these villagers were preliterate. If they were in their thirties or forties, they had not had occasion to go to primary school in their village. We could not use charts with Swahili words on them, so we used many large line or stick drawings, or found objects, or representative colors. Village leaders had a great sense of the symbolic and could immediately relate to selecting a piece of colored cloth that represented the economic state of their village. Green and red: there is a new harvest coming, just showing green, but we don't know how much we will get at the market for it, so I also choose red for my anger at the low prices! Yellow: the sun is shining here as we learn. Blue for the sky: we are aiming high. Brown for the soil: we are farmers with our fingers in the earth. They clearly felt safe in speaking their minds and hearts to one another.

Community Themes

To hear the themes of a community in a listening survey, by living there and being with the people, demanded more Swahili skills than either of us possessed. Makame could do that, and in the villages where he was accepted he could listen and reflect back to the leaders what he had heard. In other villages, and especially in parishes, his being a Muslim made it unsafe for him to be present in that way to the community. Some of the parish groups went to the bishop to complain that a Muslim was coming to teach them. We soon discovered how uncomfortable it is not to have the safety needed for learners to learn or for teachers to teach.

In one village in Musoma where we had been invited to teach the local leaders communications and management skills, we discovered an appalling polarization between the men and women. Men simply had no time for the women leaders, who had been elected by their peers. The men refused to listen to women when they spoke during the course. When women's groups made their reports, the men would talk to one another. One old man in particular, Amos, was impatient with our approach when we insisted on their listening to the women.

"Let us get on with the seminar," he said at one point. "She is just wasting our time. After all, she is only a woman." These same men could speak very warmly about democracy and equality as political party leaders and Christian teachers. Apparently they were not aware of their attitude toward their mothers, wives, and daughters.

If we had been using monologue, we would have given them a stirring lecture in carefully chosen language about *ujamaa*, the national theme of brotherhood (*sic*) and respect for all. We would have invited their questions and gone home feeling justified in the quality of our teaching. We were trying to use dialogue, however, and a good number of the principles and practices described in this book. We took a chance by using a simulated problem to catch the attention of men and women alike. I felt entirely safe doing this simple simulation, knowing that the women would come up with some way to save the situation.

The simulation began when my colleague entered the round, thatched hut where the village course was being held. She was rather agitated and asked to meet all the women in the middle of the room. The men sat quietly around the walls wondering. The teacher explained, in a concerned voice, that a child of the village had fallen into a large pit and it was impossible to get him out. He was a tiny lad of four and was terrified in the dark hole. What could be done? Outside we could hear the distant wailing of a child. Mr. Makame was providing sound effects.

The first response from the women was: "Let us call the men!" "No use!" replied the teacher. "All of the men have gone into town to watch a football game. There are no men in the village at this time." "Then let us go and call them from town!" "No, there is not enough time. The child is very frightened. We have to do something immediately." Makame, outside, wailed louder. The village women entered the role play with great gusto, making various suggestions, almost all of them indicating their dependency on the men. The village men sat by and chuckled in delight at the drama. "We can find a ladder at the carpenter's shop." The wailing continued. "We can search for a long rope! The fishermen have one!" "We can go to the next village and call their men!" Then one of the women, in a very small voice, said: "We could use our *kangas* (shawls) and make a rope!" "Yes, we could tie all of our *kangas* together and make a rope long enough to pull him out of the pit!" More wailing!

With great glee, the village women whipped off their individual shawls, made of sturdy cotton, and began with feverish haste to tie them together, forming a long rope that was thrown out the door of the hut. A great cheer arose, from men and women alike in the hut, when we pulled in the frightened, lost child (a smiling, silent Mr. Makame).

In immediate reflection upon the activity, as the women laughingly recovered their *kangas*, we began with an open question: "What happened here?" One woman responded: "We discovered a way for ourselves, without the men! We used our own resources! We made it work! We worked together!" Then the teacher asked: "Whose idea was it to use the *kangas*?" One woman replied: "It was Maria's idea, but she had only one *kanga*!"

The next morning, old Amos came to me grumbling: "You! Last night, I could not sleep thinking of those women and their *kangas*!" The women had taught the men something very important, and they had taught themselves something even more important. Our job was to design and present the task, a simulation, a role play, in a safe, structured environment, and invite their wise analysis.

Evaluation

Months afterward I happened to visit that village, and the women, seeing me, called out laughing, "We remember the *kangas*!" The safety we felt in that community had permitted us to deal with a sensitive problem through that simulation. There was no immediate indication of change in the men's relation to the women. This problem was so deep-seated in the culture that we could do nothing further about it. But the women had made a safe beginning. The old man's sleep was disturbed by this new concept. That might be the only possible indicator of success.

Ultimately, the suspicions that billowed around Mr. Makame made it impossible for him to continue working with us. (His two-year contract with CUSO was continued through other development enterprises.) We had never really made it safe enough with the community to include him in the program. We learned a hard lesson about program development: community organizing, assiduous preparation, personal contacts with key individuals and groups in a community, all are necessary to establish a safe environment for community education. Even then, the issues facing a community often have such deep cultural roots that building awareness on certain issues may be unacceptable or unsafe.

Perhaps adult learning is always dangerous. A fifty-year-old woman in one of our programs in North Carolina, investigating a welcoming undergraduate program for women at a small southern college, told the admissions officer: "My husband says he is glad for me to go back to school, as long as I do not change!" It was not safe for the husband to have his wife in college. As I look back on this Tanzanian program, I think of Donald Oliver's brilliant distinction (1989, p. 63) between technical and ontological knowledge: "Technical knowledge refers to adaptive, publicly transferable information or skills; ontological knowing refers to a more diffuse apprehension of reality, in the nature of liturgical or artistic engagement. In this latter sense, we come to know with our whole body, as it participates in the creation of significant new occasions—occasions which move from imagination and intention to critical self-definition, to satisfaction and finally to perishing and new being." I am aware that in our small, precarious community education program in Musoma, Tanzania, we were dealing almost all the time with ontological knowing. I have learned much from that experience, but mostly that safety in the learning situation, for teacher and learner, is even more necessary when we are facing the complex challenges involved in advancing ontological knowing in a cross-cultural situation.

Design Challenges

- In your own teaching and learning situations, with adults or others, how do you see safety as a variable you can control and assure? What can you do to make sure it is available to you as teacher and to others?

- What do you discern in this story as our worst move of all? That is, what seemed to lead to a loss of safety and the loss of Mr. Makame's services in the development education program?

- Why do you think the Swahili proverb—*Kupotea njia ndiko kujua njia!* (By losing the way one learns the way!)—is relevant here?

5

Sound Relationships: The Power of Friendship and Respect

In a recent study of those variables that made literacy programs work with adult students, it was dramatically shown that the relationship between the instructor and the learner was the most important factor in the learning process. I name this principle *a sound relationship*—which implies that there is friendship, but no dependency; fun without trivialization of the learning; dialogue between men and women who feel themselves peers.

The Problem and the Setting

The quality of the relationship between teacher and adult learner is the central principle in this story. I went to Indonesia in 1988 to do a two-week training of Save the Children staff on the island of Java. The training was difficult, as all learning tasks had to be translated into Indonesian and then the responses translated back into English. The end result was quite rewarding, however, as one of the Indonesian staff, a gifted artist, put the concepts and principles of community education into symbolic paintings representing Indonesian metaphors that caught the ideas being taught.

The Learners

This artist, Margie Ahnan, is an Indonesian medical doctor who two years later found herself in the United States, at a large school of public health, somewhat frustrated by the academic rendering of community health education. Her adviser at the university mentioned that there was one person in the United States she should meet: Jane Vella of Jubilee Popular Education Center in Raleigh. Margie was amazed at the synchronicity of the reference and called me at once.

Jubilee has a fellowship program that invites international students of community education to come to Raleigh and work closely with us for three months. I invited Margie to take this fellowship. She accepted with alacrity and soon arrived in Raleigh. How does one organize a three-month program for an Indonesian medical doctor so that she can go back to Indonesia and teach other health professionals how to use these principles and practices? What is the operative principle in this situation?

The Program and the Process

Our one great advantage was the informality of the situation. We set the boundaries. Margie had just come from two years of a graduate school program that she had found largely irrelevant. She is a brilliant student and a gifted artist. We sat together to design our program from the draft I presented. I showed her our calendar of training and educational events for the three months and told her what I hoped she would add to each. She was excited at the immediacy of engagement in community education.

After offering her a long reading list and suggesting she select the book she wanted to start with, we set up a daily seminar to discuss the book and any other items she was learning. I was, during these seminars, to learn a great deal about the Indonesian perspective on concepts from the texts. I was not the "professor" during these dialogues. The authors of the book were doing the teaching, and we were examining together the significance of what they had to offer. It was a rich learning experience for both of us.

The fellowship involved helping design and lead whatever workshops Jubilee was conducting during those three months. For example, we had a staff development workshop with a local hospice group. Margie sat with me to do telephone interviews with some of the hospice staff for a learning needs assessment, helped decide what we would include, prepared charts, and designed a useful longitudinal evaluation instrument. Her perspective on the hospice team's efforts, as a physician, was welcomed by our clients. She was co-facilitator with me during the program, and we could offer one another comments on our different styles and use of the principles.

After the first week, the role distinction of teacher/student began to dissolve. We were friends. There was a distinct generation gap, of course, but no gap in the acceptance of the learning potential of this experience for both of us. As Freire reminds us: "Only the student can name the moment of the death of the professor." And I would add: "But the professor has to welcome that moment in order to surely die as professor."

In our developing relationship as friends, we were able to examine each "limit situation" in the program with openness and struggle with our different perspectives without guilt or shame. Every educational program is a limit situation: it is not perfect. As we made and remade her program, we discovered our own value systems anew. I did not agree with many of Margie's perspectives on women's roles, on task allotment, on the use of class distinctions. She did not agree with many of my perspectives on task priority, on egalitarian relationships, on the teacher's role. In the struggle, we both learned. We so honored one another that it was not only necessary but possible to "hold the opposites."

The relaxed atmosphere during the three months of her fellowship—with external pressures met together, with laughter and tennis and long, leisurely meals where conversation went late into the night, with friends coming from all parts to meet this exciting Jubilee Fellow and share in the learning and teaching—was a vital part of the design. Our relationship enabled Margie to learn; it also helped Margie to teach during the Jubilee Fellowship so that her learning was confirmed later in her own cultural setting. She did not have to abandon her Indonesian perspective. She did not have to fit into an acceptable pattern or keep quiet when she heard something disagreeable. The advantages of a one-on-one mentoring situation are many. There is immediacy, as questions are answered or issues confronted as they arise. There is complete engagement, as the program is designed to meet the learning needs of one person. Most of all there is time, as the person not only spends time alone but has full access to the mentor. There is the opportunity for disagreement, in a friendly relationship that not only allows but invites honest opposition. We saw how right the poet William Blake was when he said: "Opposition is true friendship." In such a relationship we could address errors in judgment and logic, challenge incomplete thinking, and defend and celebrate cultural distinctions.

This experience for Margie was such a far cry from the graduate school program that she challenged me to test ways to introduce these variables into the formal school setting. The principle is this: the relationship of mentor to adult learner is productive of learning. Within that relationship, the variables we can control are time, affirmation, mutual respect, open dialogue, open questions that invite dialogue, engagement in significant work, role clarification, responsibility, and immediate response to questions and issues that are raised.

The one-on-one Jubilee Fellowship arrangement is one approach to getting all these variables into action. How can we structure a classroom or a workshop or an orientation or a training to bring all these variables into play? We know they work. How can we design our adult learning events so they work for us and the learners? Here are some practical suggestions for getting this relationship to work.

Time is paramount. In a graduate course at the University of North Carolina School of Public Health, I arrange to be present one hour before class to meet one or more of the graduate students for reflection or response to questions. I maintain that I am an 800 number, and they should call me whenever they are stuck. "Don't stay stuck!" I schedule potluck dinners and picnics so we have leisure time to talk. In a workshop, I schedule lunches and dinners with people so we can develop a relationship for future mutual support. In an orientation program, we set up pairs of new workers and oldtimers who mentor one another through the program. They often take time with one another after hours.

A hospice director in North Carolina, with over fifty people on staff, has devised a support system that enables relationships for learning and development to grow. Every three months, half of the staff put their names in a bowl and the other half pulls out one name. These pairs are the mutual support teams for the next three months. What they do and how they do it is entirely up to them. Their only charge is to "take care of one another." The relationships that develop, as nurses care for secretaries, doctors care for nurses, technicians take the executive director to lunch when she is feeling down, are amazing representations of the power of human beings to care when the scale is human and the structure is safe. This caring takes time. We have to be creative in finding other ways to structure such time when we are dealing with many adult learners. This creativity is part of our task as teachers of adults.

Affirmation, lavish affirmation, is possible at every step of the way, whether with large numbers of learners or small groups. Here the issue is not time or scale. It is the willingness of the "professor" to affirm at every level, to celebrate learning when you see it happening, to say, "Well done!" We can structure affirmation into a program by using force-field analysis for evaluation all the time: What did you find most useful in this session? Why? What would you suggest we change? Why?

Force-field analysis assumes there is something to celebrate and something to improve in any human endeavor. Instead of marking what is wrong on a paper or pointing out flaws in a performance, we begin by celebrating what is right. This is an attitude that must be taught to teachers of adults and practiced by them. How does one affirm what one does not agree with? I can always find it within me to say: "I honor the fact that you felt comfortable enough to say what you just said. I celebrate your strength. I do not agree with what you say and would love to argue with you about it." Affirmation is not always affirmation of the idea, but always of the person. The purpose of affirmation is to have the person learn and develop. We can never control what another person thinks. We can nurture their thinking power by affirmation and build a learning relationship.

Mutual respect can best be structured by avoiding activities that deny it: gossip, judging, "plops" (failing to acknowledge a statement or response), misrepresenting what another has said. This is often a question of tone, as well. In the diverse cultural settings where I found myself, I learned early on that tone carries meaning. Simple courtesies of language "Please," "Thank you," "If you will . . ."—carry all the more importance when they come from the "professor."

Carl Jung insisted that all those who wish to be clinical analysts (counselors) should themselves undertake a long, arduous program of analysis. Only such an experience would afford the mutuality he knew was necessary for a successful relationship between analyst and analysand. The same holds true in the adult learning process. We teachers have to honor our own need to learn and talk about it honestly. This is the greatest respect we can offer adult learners.

Re-spectare is the root of the word respect. It means: to see again. I suggest it also implies hearing again. Listening without interrupting is a simple structure for assuring respect. We can do that even in large groups. Open dialogue can readily be structured in any event: teaching a complex concept, practicing a skill, or learning an attitude. Concepts can be presented as open systems—as the hypotheses they actually are—and the adult learner can be invited to examine them, edit and add to them from their experience, do something with them. Such a dialogue builds a relationship that inevitably leads to learning and development. Donald Oliver's distinction between technical and ontological knowing, mentioned in Chapter Four, can be "taught" via open dialogue with adult learners organized in small task groups. The learning task could be:

examine this distinction between technical and ontological knowledge as described by Oliver.

1. Name one learning experience when you felt what you learned was definitely technical knowing.
2. Name one event when you felt you were engaged in ontological knowing.
3. How could you imagine a synthesis of these two events in your own life?

Share these three tasks in pairs. Then at your table share one thing you learned by doing these three tasks. We'll share a sample in the large group.

In this learning task, the relationship for learning and development is not only between the teacher and the adult learner but, more significant, within the learning pair. When we look in Chapter Eleven at a new role for the professor, we will examine the dilemma faced by the teacher here. What is the teacher's role while the adult learners are learning and developing through a well-designed learning task? This is where the poet John Keats's great concept of negative capability is helpful. Without the ability to not intrude, to wait, to be patient, to be on call, accessible as a resource, the "professor" cannot be a catalyst for this quality of learning. This is not easy. At one point in the fast-developing fellowship, Margie was designing charts, reading her books, preparing tasks for a design for an upcoming program, and writing her journal while I sat by somewhat bemused. I asked: "Just what's my role in all this?" She smiled: "Just be there, Jane, just be there!" That calls for negative capability.

During a high-intensity graduate class at the School of Public Health, small groups were working industriously and somewhat loudly on a learning task. I was in the corner of the room working just as industriously at my laptop computer. The department head looked in and asked with a smile, "Why are they always so excited?" I replied confidently, "I think, Jim, it's because they are learning." Another example, from that same graduate course, comes from a day when the learning task took three hours. I sat in the corner and told the group I would visit task groups only on request, offer my response to their questions, and leave. At the end of three hours I had had one request, which took five minutes to deal with. I had to confess to the group that it was the hardest graduate class I had ever taught. Negative capability is not easily learned. It is essential, however, in the development of sound relationships for learning and in the use of truly open dialogue.

Nonjudgmental discussion, like open dialogue, is not easy to design and implement. This is where the modeling of the professor can establish an ethical standard in the group that prevails throughout the course. Judging stops spontaneity. We have good evidence of this from everyday life. In working with adult learners, who have often suffered from judgmental bosses, spouses, in-laws, ministers, sons and daughters, the connotation of a judging remark is immense. Here again, the relationship has to be built by avoiding judgment. When Margie Ahnan made suggestions that were clearly based on an Indonesian perspective, I carefully affirmed them, argued if need be, but tried very hard not to judge them as right or wrong, good or bad. What, after all, did I know about Indonesia or the emerging perspective of its cultures? How could I judge anyway? Here again is a call for negative capability: simply avoiding judging, waiting for more information, listening. I said earlier in this book: we teach the way we were taught. We also judge the way we are judged. The only way to break the cycle is through the practice of nonjudgmental discussion, arguing with affirmation. We can structure it into our teaching/learning designs and more important, model it in our relationship with adult learners.

Open questions that invite dialogue are a simple format for building confidence, creating a relationship for learning and developing and listening. We all understand the difference between a closed question—that calls for a yes or no reply or a single-word response—and an open question that invites dialogue. The learning tasks set earlier in relation to the concepts of technical and ontological knowing were open questions. An open question invites reflection, consideration of cultural, gender, age, and personal values, and awareness of implications. In practicing a computer skill: "What do you think might happen if you deleted a paragraph before saving it? What might it mean for your work?" In learning an attitude: "Suppose you were a young lawyer and you had the chance to clerk with Thurgood Marshall when he was in the Supreme Court. Your parents are hostile to African Americans. So you turn down the chance. How would you feel today?" It takes time and effort for an educator of adults to design appropriate and provocative open questions in order to invite significant dialogue. Many of us grew up on closed questions that were answered in the back of the book. Our personal response was not invited; neither was honest dialogue. Open questions are the single sure practice that invites critical thinking and effective learning. Open questions invite me, and my peers among adult learners, to listen with mutual respect. Listening can be said to come from the Latin *oboedire*: to stand in front of what is said. We get our word *obedience* from that phrase. Who is obedient to whom in a relationship full of mutual respect? This is another example of the role transformation that can occur when we strive for a healthy relationship for learning.

Engagement in significant work and responsibility is, of course, a practical manifestation of a trusting relationship. This can be structured by designing an orientation, a training, a course, or any learning event so that adult learners are doing something of meaning to them. Again, this does not depend on one-on-one teaching. Small groups can take on learning tasks, meaningful to them, with immediate usefulness to them, and be mentors to one another in the doing of the task, in the learning. This aspect of building a strong relationship is related to the principle of engagement. Kurt Lewin (1951) made it very clear in his research that learners learned only when they were actively engaged, whether cognitively, affectively, or physically.

When Dr. Ahnan was invited to design the charts for a program, or design a learning task and lead it with a group, or prepare an evaluation instrument and test it within a learning event, she was herself learning. The task itself was her teacher. The engagement was the way she learned: by doing it. What is our role when learners are engaged in significant work? Again, with a strong dose of negative capability, our role is to be a resource, to set the task clearly without ambiguity, to make sure there are adequate physical resources to do it successfully, and to get out of the way. This engagement is not an examination. This is not a vicarious activity to test knowledge, skills, or attitudes. This is why I am specific about engagement in *significant* work. We build a strong relationship when the adult learners understand, by the structure of the design, that we expect them to do the important job well. We are there while they are doing it. We have structured it and set up the tasks they need to do, but we do not do it for them. We sit still, pay attention, and keep quiet. That is our role in the relationship at such a time.

Role clarification is a key aspect of building a strong relationship. When adult learners, in a large group or a one-on-one situation, are clear about their role, the tasks they will have to achieve to fulfill that role, and the boundaries, they can get on with the learning. When there is any ambiguity about their role, about those tasks or those boundaries, you know you are in for trouble. With Dr. Ahnan, we made clear at the beginning of the Jubilee Fellowship that her role was that of student. It was a time-bound role and she had paid for the privilege of working at Jubilee as a Fellow. She was the one who decided how she spent her time. But when she decided to take part in a program and agreed to design charts, or make an evaluation instrument, or lead a session, she could be held responsible to do just that. We signed an agreement to this effect.

In terms of what she did and when she did it in the Jubilee Fellowship, she had the deliberative voice. As an adult learner in this fellowship program, she was the decision maker. I had a consultative voice and could make suggestions about her program. But it was her program. When she decided to take part in a Jubilee program, the roles reversed. I had the deliberative voice and she had a consultative one. This clarification kept us safely apart, so we were not in one another's way, and kept us working smoothly together. It made for assured accountability on both sides, as well. I was accountable to Margie—to make suggestions, to be a mentor. She was accountable to herself and to Jubilee when she decided to work in a program. As a Jubilee Fellow, she was not accountable to me except in basic human courtesies and as a guest in a strange culture. I was accountable to her. Here is another point of transformation of the paradigm in adult learning. In traditional educational programs, the master is in charge and the students are accountable to him. In this approach to adult learning, however, these roles reverse. It makes all the difference. It is what Thomas Kuhn calls a "paradigm shift" (Kuhn, 1970), and it is, in my experience, the genesis of healthy relationships for learning and development.

Immediate response to questions that are raised is an aspect of that accountability. How can this occur when you are working with a large number of adults? We need to creatively design structures that make this happen. Immediacy has been proven to be one of the basic aspects of adult learning. When an issue is hot, it is hot. Waiting to deal with it later risks the loss of a learning moment. Here are some structures that have worked in large groups to honor immediacy:

- Set the norm that any question which arises has priority over the task at hand. This means that adult learners are invited to interrupt the learning task to ask their question or raise their burning issue. This is not often easy to accept, as it can look like the proverbial red herring. But in my experience, one adult's question is often the unformulated question of the whole group. It is useful to refer such a question to the group by what I call a bouncing question. "Before I respond, what do you think of Mary's question?" This continues the vital peer learning while leaving time for you to respond in full.

You as teacher are thus developing a relationship for learning among peers.

- Structured time can be set before and after a session so that immediate concerns can be dealt with in dialogue. Other structured time can be set when the teacher is accessible outside the class.

- The proverbial 800 number is another way to deal with immediate issues. The onus is on the teacher to respond as quickly as possible to a question. If this does not happen the 800 number will not be used again.

- I use my fax machine to deal with issues when clients or students are designing programs. We need not talk at all. They send me their draft designs or papers or whatever, and I make my notes on the draft and simply send it right back. This is a useful instrument for immediate response and feedback, confirming a relationship of mutual trust.

Capturing the learning moment is what all these structures aim at doing. We all have had the awesome experience of being present at a learning moment: the *aha*! moment, the time when the concept is realized, when the abstract word becomes flesh! I know that moment by the quality of the silence that pervades the room, whether it is filled with a thousand or a hundred or ten adults or just two of us. The quality of silence is a symbol of what Joseph Campbell (1972) calls a moment of "transparent transcendence." How many times in that Jubilee Fellowship did Margie and I enjoy that quality of silence? How many times did we have that experience in that three-month period? As a teacher in the formal school system for twenty years, I may have heard that once or twice. Today, using this popular education approach to adult learning, I live that moment, through these relationships, once or twice daily.

Evaluation

From her position as a physician in Indonesia, Dr. Ahnan tells me she uses this approach in teaching public health nurses how to work with Indonesian women and their children. Her descriptive phrase for the results is a culturally apt metaphor: "These nurses are now sharing their own strengths, using all the principles of popular education with the women. The tigers are loose in Java!"

Design Challenges

No matter what your engagement as an adult educator, administrator, designer of programs, teacher, or evaluator may be, the principle of building a healthy relationship can help.

- Consider one person with whom you have a constant interaction: a colleague, a peer, a secretary, a student, a boss. Take some time now to consider how you can design a system to support a relationship for learning and development by including all the aspects discussed in this chapter: time, affirmation, mutual respect, open dialogue, open questions that invite dialogue, engagement in significant work, responsibility, role clarification, immediate response to questions that are raised.

- What else would you add to this set of strategies from your unique culture and personality? Your own cultural perspectives will offer the most useful and successful strategies. Whatever the strategy, your unique personal style must be honored.

6

Sequence and Reinforcement: Knowing Where and How to Begin

Sequence and reinforcement are a set of principles that work remarkably well in language learning—and in every other kind of teaching as well. A rare sequence of events led to a call from Dr. Tito Craige, an old friend. Would I be willing to work with him to train young college students to teach Haitian migrant workers English through the Migrant and Seasonal Farm Workers organization (MSFW)?

Tito and I were old friends from North Carolina State University, where he had burst into my office one morning to ask:

"Are you Dr. Vella?"

"I am!"

"Well, you have the most interesting reserve shelf of books in the library!"

Tito had been browsing during a long day of research on his doctoral dissertation and had wandered over to the reserve shelves and seen my collection for my graduate course on popular education. Such a delightful and innovative meeting was only the beginning of more delightful and innovative encounters. This May telephone call offered great possibilities.

The Problem and the Setting

Tito explained his dream: a mobile classroom that would drive to migrant labor camps, equipped with all the materials and technology that would help workers learn what they needed to know: English, coping skills for entrance into a new society, how to get and keep a green card, all the skills, knowledge, and attitudes a migrant worker wanted. He had funds for the mobile classroom and permission from growers to come into the camps. What he needed now was a well-trained teacher corps, a group of skilled men and women familiar with the principles of adult learning, to do the job.

"Tito," I apologized, "I have never even been inside a migrant camp! I have never met a migrant worker! How in the world can I teach young people how to teach migrant workers English? Let me make a deal with you. I will spend this summer teaching in a migrant camp in your program. This will provide me with the experiential base I need to speak with authority to the young people who want to be in this teacher corps."

The sequence here is vital: I could have designed a training course and then gone to the camps, or I could have designed and led a training course and then checked it out by observing the teachers at work in the camps. But I thought I should learn the situation and the environment first and then design and lead the training. Tito agreed with some reluctance, since he had wanted to do the training before the summer session. He set me up with a group of Haitian migrant workers to teach them literacy skills and English every Tuesday evening from 7 to 9. I attended the short orientation program for new teachers and set forth.

The Learners

I drove to McGees Crossroads with some trepidation the first night. How would I present myself to these Haitian migrant workers? They had come to supplement the Mexican workforce and had to face not only a strange new world but also the antagonism of their fellow workers in the fields, who naturally felt threatened by this new group. What would be the wisest first step for me to take? In the orientation we had heard all the history and legal aspects of the migrant situation in the early 1980s. Yet it still was not clear to me. I knew these men were here without their families whom they had left in Haiti. They had been hired for this one single summer and were obliged to be back in Haiti by the end of the year. They would pick tobacco and vegetables in North Carolina through August and then follow the vegetable harvest stream up through Michigan before leaving in the fall.

They had to learn English, not only to survive, but even to consider a future possibility of immigrating, getting a green card, and becoming a citizen. Of course, I knew no Creole and it had been at least ten years since I had used my French. This was going to be action learning: complete physical response or nothing. A young man from MSFW who did know Creole met me at the camp and introduced me to the gathered group of nine young Haitian men. We stood on the back porch of a wooden shack, their home while they picked tobacco and cotton for this grower. We had driven through the tiny southern town of McGees Crossroads and white folks there had glowered unhappily when they saw my car pull into the dirt road that led to the migrant camp. What was I doing there with "them"?

The Program and the Process

Sequence means begin at the beginning: move from small to big, slow to fast, easy to hard. We all know that. What, in this case, was small? What was slow? What was easy? As I watched the pickup truck of the MSFW representative blow dust into the evening sky on his way to another camp, I turned shyly to the expectant group of men. I smiled. They smiled. We all leaned on the rails of the porch. There were no chairs. I laughed nervously. They laughed. Finally I said, in English, "My name is Jane. How can I say that in Creole?" Jean Pierre, who knew a little English, translated my question to the group. Everyone talked at once. Finally through the static I heard a pattern and tried to say what I had heard. "*Minom ez Jeanne.*" They laughed even harder! Again they gave me the phrase in slow, sure Creole. Again I tried. The laughter rose. It was not laughter at me, it was sheer delight in the spectacle of this educated, gray-haired woman making such a mash out of three little words!

I gave up on my efforts at self-identification and asked Jean Pierre (in English): "How do you say in Creole: 'Good evening? How are you?' " He told me and I tried. Side-splitting laughter, deep belly chuckles, high fives to one another accompanied by broad smiles! I tried again. And again. The laughter quieted as one by one the men tried to help me with the various sounds, repeating them for me in isolation as I struggled to get my tongue around them.

Finally, I was too tired to try any more. I wiped my sweating brow, swatted one of the million mosquitoes that were feasting on this language class, and said: "Gentlemen, start your engines. You see how difficult it is for anyone to learn a new language!" So we began with simple greetings in English, going around the porch, one by one, working in pairs to ask and respond, moving in a very slow sequence from "Hello, how are you?" "I'm fine, thanks" to a few basic everyday phrases.

I did not know if they could read and write, so I asked each man to write on a clean paper the name of his wife or mother or sweetheart in Port au Prince or wherever home was in Haiti. Some wrote easily, others asked their friends to write, some wrote with great difficulty. Noting where each one was, I immediately formed learning teams, one writer on each team.

By now they were sitting on the floor of the back porch with notebooks on their laps and stubby pencils in their hands. Here was a high-tech learning lab in McGees Crossroads. I asked them each to find something in the house they would like to send to the person whose name they had written. They dashed into the shack and came out with transistor radios, a tin of Campbell's soup, a watch, a clock, a pillow from their bed. These were our first vocabulary words. I modeled for them a simple repetition exercise. I took one man's object: *a clock*. They repeated the word, holding and feeling the object, which they passed around the porch. "Marie, Marie!" (Jean Pierre had written his fiancée's name, Marie.) They smiled as they read the name written on Jean Pierre's paper. "I will send. I will send," they repeated with alacrity. "I will send Marie a clock! He will send Marie a clock! Jean Pierre will send Marie a clock!" They laughed in joy at their sudden command of this elusive language! Each held up his object, and we went the round with: *a pillow.* "Annette. I will send Annette a pillow! He will send Annette a pillow! Antoine will send Annette a pillow!" We moved happily on through Angela, Moisette, Jeanne Marie, Giselle, and a lamp, a can of soup, a watch, a ring.

The ring got the loudest response and a great deal of teasing in Creole. Young Roberto blushed brightly under his dark skin as the group sang out: "Roberto will send Giselle a ring!" The reinforcement of the single pattern, over and over again, with variations provided by the affective response with new names and new objects, gave them control over that phrase. It was not perhaps the most useful phrase for their daily speech, but it held deep affect that would make them repeat it themselves at times. In our synthesis, at the end of the two-hour session, each man was able to say proudly: "Hello, my name is Jean Pierre. How are you? I'm fine, thanks. I will send Marie a clock!" His fellows shouted their praise as each man proved what he had learned.

The next week, I arrived a bit after seven. The nine men were on the back porch, dressed as if to go to a formal event. Shoes shined, white shirts sparkling, trousers so pressed you could cut yourself on the crease. They greeted me with their chorus of English phrases. "Hello, how are you? I'm fine, thanks!" The sounds had become a bit confused, but these phrases had clearly been practiced over the week. They knew the principle of reinforcement. We continued taking small steps, using more found objects, and continuing to connect to their families in Haiti. We worked in teams, writing and reading the English words we had practiced speaking. Progress seemed excruciatingly slow to me. In their eyes, however, they were taking giant steps, adding to their repertoire of phrases and sentences they knew they knew. I am convinced that fidelity to the principle of sequence is harder on the teacher than on the adult learner.

We spent a great deal of time on the back porch beating out the time of the phrases and sentences they were learning. "I will send Marie this clock!" Part of the sequence in language learning is hearing the idiosyncratic rhythms of the language in question. We did this by drumming on the door and walls of the back porch of their sleeping house for much of the summer until I could hear they had some control of the rhythm of the language.

A Bloody Immediate Evaluation

One evening I arrived to discover that Jean Pierre was not present. I asked about him and was told he had had two teeth extracted that day. I offered my sympathy and got on with the lesson. Suddenly, in the doorway, Jean Pierre appeared. His face was the color of old parchment, and he held a cooking pot in one hand and a wet face-cloth over his lips. He greeted me respectfully and sat down on the floor of the porch with his colleagues. He could not talk, of course, and interrupted our drumming and singsong of phrases with his coughing blood into the pot. Should I tell him he did not have to be there? Jean Pierre, however, was the subject of his own learning. He had made a decision. He would attend this class, and I could only celebrate his decision. He sat there throughout the class, utterly attentive, listening, smiling as well as he could in his pain, pouring blood into the cooking pan. Some indicators of success in teaching are more moving than others.

In their sense of sequence, these Haitian language students set up protocols for class night. If I arrived at seven and they had had a long day in the tobacco fields, one would come onto the back porch and visit with me while the others showered and dressed. They never came to class in anything but their Sunday-go-to-meeting clothes. If anyone were to visit our back porch language lab, they surely would have suspected that I, in my casual dress, was the migrant worker and the men were sophisticated language consultants from the Caribbean.

Evaluation of Community Response

At one point in this summer program, I decided to try to get the neighbors in McGees Crossroads to join me in my effort at language teaching. They could reinforce our program best by providing a more human and functional site for the class than the rickety, mosquito-infested back porch. I wrote to the mayor of McGees Crossroads, telling him of our venture and indicating that I had seen, in passing, a classroom in the back of the local fire station. How about letting us use that classroom every Tuesday night from 7 to 9? I had a quick response: "Dear Dr. Vella. We use that room every evening. Sorry."

I had to learn that the arrival of Haitian migrant workers in a small North Carolina town was part of a whole social and cultural history. I could not break the sequence of that southern reality. As a friend of mine pointed out, "Jane, you will never be invited to a pig pickin' in McGees Crossroads!" I recall another friend offering me wise advice when I, as a young woman, was heading to Tanzania. I had asked her what advice she would give me if she thought I would take it. "Reserve judgment, Jane, for the first ten years!" I see now how this too is related to sequence. It is so easy to think that we teachers of adult learners have grasped the whole situation and, having done a learning needs assessment, know all there is to know about what must be learned and taught. I have learned that every needs assessment has to be open at both ends: there may be more we need to know about the genesis of the situation—and more they need to know than we can teach. Sequence is a useful principle that is never completely used up during a program.

Evaluation

Newly confident that I knew something about the situation these young men and women were getting into, I designed and led the training for the next year's teachers. Tito and I wrote a book for the new teachers and I dedicated it to my own teachers: the Haitian migrant workers I had met on the back porch in McGees Crossroads. The migrant workers followed the stream of ripening vegetables into New England that summer, and many wove themselves into the workforce of their adopted nation as a result of their new-found language skill.

My stories of Jean Pierre and his colleagues gave the new teachers in training lots of laughs and some encouragement that they too could use sequence and reinforcement to enable these courageous men to learn the language that could secure their entrance into a new life. Knowing English, knowing how to read and write, would make a world of difference.

Design Challenges

- Take any lesson you have planned: a class, a workshop, a seminar. Examine it for the occasions of reinforcement of your primary concept, skill, or attitude. How often do you repeat the idea in a new way—to keep the engagement of the learner, to emphasize the importance of the central point? Remember the magic number: 1,142. That's how many times, I am convinced, I need to hear or do something before I know I know it.

- A principle is the beginning of an action. The principle of sequence invites us to examine our actions and organize them anew if the principle is not working. None of these principles works in isolation. We can readily see that our sequence is not working for an adult learner when he looks confused or lost. This kind of physical indicator gives you the information you need as teacher to change your sequence with that individual or group. Stop now to reflect on a situation where an adult learner was simply not getting something you were trying to teach. Look at the one learner. Look at your program. How could you change the distance between steps in the sequence to get that learner on board with the necessary confidence? How could you affirm and reinforce what he has already accomplished?

- The size of a group is directly related to the potential for effective reinforcement and the quality of sequence. In this migrant labor camp I was fortunate to have a one-digit classroom: nine, not ten, adult learners. I am personally convinced that the one-digit classroom (nine, not ten) has tremendous potential not only for adult language learning but for the formal school system as well. Imagine the reinforcement and the personalized sequence of learning tasks that are possible in a one-digit classroom. It is an idea whose time has come.

- The principles of popular education are so interwoven it is impossible not to see many at work in a situation. Two other principles that are manifest in this story of the migrant labor camp in North Carolina: humor and rhythm. Again, consider any teaching you are presently doing. What was hilariously funny? How can you celebrate that? How can you bring humor into the adult learning situation? Nothing is better reinforcement than a discovery of the incongruity in a situation—the dancing light on the waters of ideas that will not fit together but dash against one another. There are endless opportunities for laughter in an adult learning situation. While rhythm lends itself obviously to language learning, consider how it could be used in helping adults learn whatever you are teaching. How could you use rhythm, poetry, dance in your adult learning classes?

7

Action with Reflection: A Lesson in Leadership

Praxis is the Greek word for action with reflection. It is a vital principle for effective adult learning. This story of a community development training event in the Maldives shows how praxis worked for all of us.

The Problem and the Setting

The Maldives is a small island republic stretching like a sandy Milky Way north-south in the Indian Ocean southwest of India and Sri Lanka. There are twenty-one atolls, each with hundreds of islands that form administrative units for the government. When Save the Children, an international community development organization, decided to offer staff and resources for community development work in the Maldives, the government proposed as an impact area the outlying northernmost atoll, Haa Alifu, largely because government personnel rarely got to visit any of the sixteen inhabited islands of the atoll. When Michael Gibbons and Karen LeBan, co-directors of the program, invited me to conduct a training program with their small staff, I was delighted.

Here was a development program, with many interagency links, working directly with various ministries of the government of the Maldives, ripe for such field training. As usual, our lengthy correspondence prior to my arrival included my request for five days on site before the training event—days to be spent with Michael and

Karen and whomever they named, reviewing the situation, doing a needs assessment, designing an appropriate training program. We stressed the need for practical work: doing what we were learning. This meant doing the workshop in the impact area or someplace where program work with communities was going on. The site named by Michael and Karen was Utheem Island, one of the islands of Haa Alifu atoll, a two-day boat trip from Male, the nation's capital.

I read all I could find about the Maldives. As in so many other instances, the agency was seen by the government of the Maldives as a resource bringing skills and funds to the island development program. The selection of such a distant impact area indicated what the government wanted: a development arm that had power and resources to reach across thousands of miles of open seas to Haa Alifu atoll. Did the government of the Maldives see this agency as an educational resource? No. They measured community development success in terms of buildings constructed, bridges reinforced, houses roofed. They had, however, recently opened a Center for Community Education and Development in Male. One of the participants in our training course, Mustafa Hussein, is an education specialist in that center. Perhaps this training event could link the concepts of development and education in a new way to catch the attention of the Maldive government. To this end, Karen and Michael sent out an announcement to all ministries of the government, to three other private voluntary organizations, and to the United Nations Development Program (UNDP), inviting them to join the training course for community development workers. Through this course they could have a new experience of doing community development through community education.

The Learners

During the five days of preparation for the workshop, I had occasion to meet some of the participants from UNDP and the government. John Galace, a bright, energetic Filipino on the UNDP staff in the Maldives, was obviously going to be an important resource to the entire training project. A young field coordinator from the Sri Lanka program of Save the Children, E. E. Wijeratne, joined us from Columbo, and three young field coordinators from the Maldives Save the Children program were waiting for us in the atoll, having made logistical preparations for our arrival. I met Mustafa Hussein. It was he who ultimately took the fruit of this training workshop and made it available to all government programs in the islands.

Three ministries were represented: Agriculture, Atolls Administration, and Fisheries. Volunteers in Service Overseas, a British group, sent their Maldivian administrative officer. Language, as always, was a major issue. All of the group discussions during the workshop would be in Divehi, the language of the Maldives. While tasks were set in English, they were all translated into Divehi. We will see how pictures with Divehi titles enabled us to extend the workshop throughout the whole island nation.

The Program and the Process

During the few days of preparation we had reserved in Male before setting out on our two-day boat trip to Utheem, we used the Seven Steps of Planning to complete a specific design for the course. We studied the profile of the participants (Who), the situation (Why), and then, considering the time frame (When) and the site near the villages (Where), we could determine the content of the training (What) and set achievement-based objectives (What For). Finally we set tasks for the participants to do in order to learn the content. As we examined the situation, we saw that the development issues in the Maldives called for training in skills and educational work with field staff to move from a construction ethic of development to a new role of empowering communities to make decisions and raise resources for their own development.

Save the Children had been addressing this change in development direction for years, and we wanted to share our insights with other nongovernmental agencies as well as with government and UN staff. As the new Center for Community Education was in the midst of a project to design a community development manual for the islands, Mustafa Hussein could certainly use what he learned here. We boldly set two simple objectives for this training as praxis. By the end of this workshop, participants would have (1) redefined and experienced anew the role and tasks of community development specialists and (2) designed, practiced, and evaluated community education for development. Mustafa remarked on reading these: "They look simple, but I expect they are not as easy as they look." Our aim was to give these people a new experience of community development as community education, a ten-day praxis that would involve action in the community with reflection.

During the praxis of the workshop, these men and women taught one another as they reflected together on their new role in the nearby village where they did a community survey and practice teaching. They came to conclusions for themselves. They knew they knew because they had just done what they were learning. On the first day, participants cited their expectations in response to a learning task: "What do you hope to learn or achieve by the end of these ten days?" They said they wanted to know how to encourage the community to develop by their own resources, how to deal successfully with people, how to share experiences for motivating poor communities, how to make other people aware of the possibility of improving their lives, how to satisfy leaders and laymen at the same time, how to solve problems they face when working with the community, how to examine and redefine their work, how to clarify their own direction. These expectations informed the two objectives. It is the teacher's responsibility to set training objectives very clearly and explicitly for participants before the training begins and then, in honest dialogue, ask them what they want to do in light of these objectives. The dialogue begins by design when we invite these expectations.

We set up an open day for rest and relaxation in the midst of the ten days. This gave us, the leaders of the workshop, the chance to redesign and reshape the workshop as needed. We used that day to organize visuals for a complete synthesis of all concepts learned in the first four days. The group artist designed pictures to represent all the concepts. Since none of us wrote Divehi, a beautiful script resembling Persian, these pictorial concepts were very useful indeed. Ultimately Mustafa Hussein produced a booklet with all these pictures and titles in Divehi.

The island site was perfect for such a training session. We were invited to use the new Mohammed Thakurufanu Memorial Center, which sat in the middle of the small island, a stone's throw from the villages where participants in the training could go to do needs assessment, listening for villagers' themes, and practice teaching. This would be excellent praxis. Each of the learning tasks we designed was a means of modeling this problem-posing approach to adult learning, which we hoped all the participants would learn and adopt. What we did in the training room is what they would do in the villages. How could they see that their best image of themselves was that of teacher of the community, a master of dialogue, and not merely mason or carpenter or bridge builder? Unless they reconsidered their role as community development specialists, the villagers' dependence on them would simply grow. Dependency, whether on foreign specialists or on national experts from the capital town of Male, eats at the heart of a development process. Their praxis in the villages had to be acting in this new relationship and reflecting on it together with the villagers and among themselves.

Three events during the ten-day training stand out as significant aspects of their doing what they learned—of their praxis. The first was community visits. In their first walk through the small community, the pairs of specialists were awkward and shy. Even Mustafa Hussein, so outgoing and talkative, was unsure what to do with the women and children they met under the shade trees around the mud and wattle houses. They reported their discomfort when they came back, and we explored new ways they could interact with the community. They tried again, and again, and each time it seemed easier and more fruitful. They heard community themes more clearly and were building a fine relationship with the small group of womenfolk they found at home each day. This was an excellent example of praxis: the action-with-reflection cycle that is a natural way of learning. Praxis is a special kind of action, full of reflection, leading to new, refined action. It is an ongoing, never-ending cycle of change toward a better situation. These Maldivian community development specialists learned about praxis through their efforts to reach the community people.

The second event involved a change of plans. On the morning after their free day—which they had spent on an open boat going to a distant island—they were not fully present to the learning tasks set out for the day. I tried to set the task and get groups started, but there was simply no energy in the group for the effort. It was 9:07 (we had started at 9 AM). "Let's take a short break," I suggested, much to everyone's surprise. The group dispersed, some to smoke in the courtyard, some to search out a cup of tea. They were confused by the "break" and murmured questioningly among themselves. I met Karen and Michael and confessed: "I do not know what to do!" After huddling a bit, we called people back to go out, two by two, into the community to search for more themes, to listen to the people, to continue their community analysis. They came back after a few hours energized and excited by what they had heard, ready to share their research, ready to get on with the workshop.

Here was an example of praxis. What had Michael and Karen and I learned? When you do not know what to do next, admit it and get some help from colleagues. When energy is low, get people into a physically active learning task in order to raise the energy for learning. Michael Gibbons told me later that this was the best lesson he had ever learned about training and adult learning. When Mustafa Hussein asked about the sudden decision to take an early break, we explained what had happened. All of the group realized, in a unique manner, the need for physical activity when the energy is low. It was a memorable lesson for us all.

The task we set for the group in order to study the concept of leadership was yet another highlight. It occurred toward the end of the workshop. The small dinghy, *The Whaler*, used to move people and goods to the larger boats offshore, lay on a sandy beach on one side of the island. Its engine had been repaired and was in the boathouse near the large jetty. The dinghy had to be brought around manually to the jetty, on the other side of the island, in order to move the group to the large boat at high tide (6 AM) on the day of departure.

This was the learning task set to the group: "We are considering the qualities of leadership. Now, our job is to move that dinghy to the jetty." Before the task was explained further, the group of twelve men and women rushed out the door. Karen, Michael, and I followed to observe signs of leadership in the group. They reached the dinghy and pushed it into the water. Three men jumped in and began to paddle with their arms. Another fellow grabbed a long pole and began to push the boat with the pole, competing for a place in the dinghy with his friends. Another man jumped into the water to push the boat, which was by then quite full. Some of the passengers jumped out and pushed with him, and those on the beach joined in. Someone hooked an anchor into the boat, and pulled the boat using the anchor rope. The long haul around the island, through the shallow water, involved almost the entire group. A bright flag was raised (someone's shirt) and the project continued with cheers and songs. At last we reached the jetty and, in a final team effort, lifted the dinghy onto the beach.

Everyone was laughing and talking excitedly as they fell, quite exhausted, onto the sand. I seized the moment to examine the "learning task." What did you see happen? Why do you think it happened this way? It was clear that haste was a self-imposed criterion for all the members of the group. Was this how they organized their community development work? Was the criterion: How soon can we get it done? Was that their measure of success as leaders? Clearly, there had been no planning at all. Action people all, they set out to do the task in whatever way possible. Time had been lost and energy wasted as the strategy changed again and again; not everyone helped, either, because people did not know their role. It was a haphazard venture at best. This action needed reflection.

What did we learn from this? As they reflected, they considered that the task of leaders is to organize, to set out shared tasks, to clarify roles, to name goals and set time limits. Leadership is not always a question of sweat. It can be a question of thought. Nothing in the workshop matched this experience for richness and potential for analysis. A video camera capturing that scene on the beach would have greatly enriched the learning potential. We could have played that tape over and over whenever we wanted to consider the responsibilities of leadership. A voice overlay in Divehi could have made it available to any leader on the islands who had a videocassette recorder. We missed that chance.

We used this praxis as an example of *their* idea of a development specialist: a person who does the job. They all realized the development specialist can also be a person who leads others, organizes them, inspires them, helps them to determine what they want to do, and shows them how to do it most effectively.

Evaluation

Mustafa Hussein and his friends learned about themselves and achieved the first objective of the workshop: to redefine and experience anew the role and tasks of a community development specialist. As we closed the workshop, we considered the next steps. Mustafa explained that the Community Education Center was preparing a pamphlet on community development in Divehi, and he promised to use these concepts in the pamphlet's design. They have since produced a community education curriculum at the center. These skills and attitudes and this knowledge helped them to put that key educational resource together.

After a stormy two-day journey in the launch back to Male, the group parted, assuring one another how they would work together. Mustafa led the coordination of a series of workshops for other ministries, assisted by Michael and Karen from Save the Children and John from UNDP, during which they taught what they had learned on Utheem. The community development booklets produced in Divehi for the entire country reflected a problem-posing, participative approach to adult learning and development. All of the concepts and skills learned on Haa Alifu atoll were included through a series of charming cartoons, making them accessible to both literate and preliterate island workers. Mustafa had been right: the objectives of the community development workshop in the Maldives had indeed been achieved. But they were not at all as simple as they looked.

This experience with a small group of community education people proved again that even the most complex concepts, and even the simplest, can be learned best by active involvement with the learning process. When the "leaders" felt embarrassed about their chaotic efforts to move the boat, and reflected on ways they could have worked more systematically, they were learning. When we finished that activity, they knew they knew. I could say with assurance that they had demonstrated problems in leadership and discovered ways to work as leaders in the community.

When Mustafa Hussein and his friends took the concepts, skills, and attitudes of the workshop, turned them into a participative workshop in Divehi, produced a picture book for development workers in the islands, and taught others, they knew they knew those concepts, skills, and attitudes. When the group discovered how intimidating their presence in the village was—and then organized to change their ways of greeting the women and talking with them—they learned how to do a community survey. Praxis offered them the experience and the opportunity to reflect on their experience together. During one of the reflection periods, Mustafa Hussein said: "We see now that change is from the heart!"

These concepts, skills, and attitudes are in the bones and muscles of the participants now. I await with anticipation further news of development processes in the Maldives. This experience could make a world of difference.

Design Challenges

In your teaching and in the design of your programs, how can you introduce praxis to energize the adult learners and invite them to significant learning? Remember that a learning task is praxis when it includes not only significant action but time for reflection on that action. Examine the following critical incident. Decide how this frustrated teacher could use praxis to bring the group to more effective learning of skills and knowledge of new computer programs.

Howard is a computer instructor at a community college. He has a large class of thirty young men and women who are being introduced to the use of the computer as a word processor. Using a popular program, Howard walks them through a series of simple steps. Although they are engaged for a while, some fall out because they got lost, while others are frankly bored by the repetition of the work. Howard gets more and more frustrated by the fact that the young people are not paying attention to his commands—not doing what he is telling them. He is working at his keyboard, using an overhead projection to demonstrate his every move. The room is dark. Finally, in somewhat of a rage, Howard tells the group: "Just watch me! We'll get to practice this later!" He then demonstrates ten vital steps in the program. The students, passive and subdued, sit and watch.

Use these Four Open Questions to learn from Howard's dilemma.

- What do you see happening here?
- Why do you think it is happening?
- If this happens when you are teaching, what problems will it cause you and the adult learners?
- What have you learned from the example in the Maldives that we might use to cure this prevailing problem in education?

8

Learners as Subjects of Their Own Learning

In this story of Durga of Nepal, we examine the principle that respects the learners as subjects or decision makers in their own learning. Nepal is a magnificently beautiful country of vast mountain ranges and rolling lowlands, with strong-legged and strong-minded people who have maintained their unique culture for millennia. The young man who is the subject of this story, Durga Bahadur Shrestha, is a striking example of the integrity and intelligence of Nepali youth.

The Problems and the Setting

The problem I faced as we began the training-of-trainers workshop was this: How can an American woman teacher invite a group of young Nepali men and women, field staff of a community development organization, to become more effective adult educators in a period of three to six weeks? One thing was sure. They would have to be decision makers, subjects, of their own learning and development. What could an outsider share with them except principles of learning that have worked in other cultures and problems of learning that face cultures the world over?

It was the German philosopher Hegel who made the distinction between being a subject—a decision maker—and being an object at the disposal of other people. This is a powerful distinction. I have observed learners from many cultures resonate with the potential of being subjects of their own lives and own learning. Perhaps this is so because many of these cultures have been dominated by other powers. We are designed as human beings to be subjects; the world is an object for us to shape and enhance. The content of a course is an object for us, learners and teacher as subjects, to examine together as we decide what is useful and true. At the completion of the second training-of-trainers course I led with field staff in Nepal, I asked the group how they thought they had changed during the two last weeks of training. Durga smiled his delightful smile and pointed proudly at himself, saying, "Subject!"

The program and projects of Save the Children in Nepal lie in an area ten to twelve hours by foot from the field office in Katmandu. Durga's task is to coordinate health education programs in Takukot, some fourteen hours from the capital. This agency often works in the more remote areas where government services are rare and the need is greatest. This means that the field staff—nurses, agriculturists, community development specialists, water engineers, housing specialists, road developers—all must be self-directed and self-monitored teamworkers who are indeed subjects of their own lives. How could a training program for professional field staff emphasize their responsibility to be decision makers (subjects) of the community development program in these Himalayan mountains of Nepal? What could we do to invite that smile and that expression of self-confidence—"Subject!"—from Durga?

Community development in Nepal is a complex affair owing to the rough terrain of the country. The glorious Himalayas are home to thousands of small communities of mountain farmers who make their living in agriculture, fishing, and livestock. This is a unique setting for learning. By *setting* I mean all those aspects of the environment that make or break the educational opportunity for learners. Distances in Nepal are major obstacles. To get a sick child to a hospital may mean a two- or three-day trek down dangerous mountain slopes. To market a crop of tomatoes, the farmer walks a vertical track to urban centers like Katmandu or Gorka. Imagine a toothache six days away from a dentist!

The community development programs in the area had matured over eight years. The staff worked with sensitivity and empathy to form a viable, durable program in the distant mountain outposts of Dhuwakot, Deurali, Pandrung, Mahjlakuribot. The Katmandu field office directed and serviced these mountain programs. In 1985, I was invited to conduct a training of trainers in popular education with field staff. I was new to Save the Children and had a great deal to learn about the settings of such training events. I did insist that the training take place in a field site so that there would be ample opportunity to do teaching practice in the villages.

On the second day of our trek into the Himalayas, we arrived at the training site: a remote and desolate mountainside a few miles north of the village of Pandrung where Save the Children had a small office. Thirty field staff from all of the mountain programs met us—with some anticipating the training and some alarmed at the prospect of two weeks in tents on the mountainside. Durga offered a warm welcome to his impact area, which had overnight become the agency's training center for Nepal.

The Sherpas set to work with experienced efficiency and prepared a tent camp: dining tent, sleeping tents spread along the sides of the mountain, kitchen tent, latrines built into the hillside. As trainer I wondered: Where in the world are we going to teach? The villages around were wonderful for practical work, but where would we gather for the training itself? Should we use the one large tent that served as a dining room? I decided that we should not. After all, we had to respect the learners' need for relaxation and distance from the training at least at mealtimes. They needed this large tent for rest and relaxation, as a gathering place, a "living room." On the way to the campsite we had passed a rather charming, if dilapidated, cow shed that looked like a scene from an old Christmas card. The roof of mud and wattle slanted to the ground; the floor was covered with dirty straw; there were no walls—one could sit on the floor and see miles and miles of Himalayan mountains, all the way toward Tibet and China. There were, furthermore, no cows in this stable. A footpath passed by the shed, used by villagers on their way to and from the little town four miles away. When I inquired, Durga explained that this stable belonged to an old farmer whose cows had all been sold.

I had immediately thought of this cow shed as a possible training site, but I knew this decision could not be mine. I was not the subject because I did not know enough about Nepali customs. The group had to decide. The learners had to be the subjects of the training even at this point. Their voice on this matter was deliberative (decision making), not merely consultative. I invited Durga and his colleagues to search out an appropriate training site in the vicinity of our camp. They left in small groups, somewhat confused by the assignment, somewhat bemused by this strange American woman in their midst. They came back to report that they had discovered an old cow shed and wanted me to look at it with them. They were apprehensive, however, that my own cultural taboos would not allow us to use an abandoned mud and wattle stable. Perhaps they did not think of the precedent in the Christian tradition. We looked at it together and decided it was not only convenient to the camp but large enough and bright enough for training work. We all agreed to clean it up at once and name it "The Place of Learning." This was a lovely Nepali phrase: *gaiko got*.

A carpet of clean straw, an easel tucked into the corner under the low roof with a large chart full of Nepali characters, a scattering of mats from the tents, and our place of learning (*gaiko got*) was ready. Their having made this decision, and my having corroborated it, got the training-of-trainers workshop off to a very good start. They experienced what it meant to be subjects, decision makers, of at least one important variable: the setting of the training. Later, when we spoke of the principle of being subjects, they could use this experience to test the authenticity of the concept. This was Durga's first explicit experience in this training of trainers. He discovered how it felt to make a decision with the group.

This is what we mean by *praxis*. We begin with experience, analyze that experience, search for new information that can inform the experience, and then change our knowledge set or behavior to incorporate the new data. *Praxis* is the Greek word for action, but it is action full of reflection by subjects. It is the opposite of impulsive, mindless action by people who see themselves as objects of others. It is the basis of learning among subjects using this approach of dialogue. How significant it was that the first action of the Nepal field staff participating in the workshop was praxis. We can use real-life situations to teach ourselves and others all the time.

The setting of this unique training of trainers in Nepal was a key variable in the workshop's success. As we saw in Chapter Three, using the Seven Steps of Planning we can respect the significance of the learning site. Where we choose to teach is a way of respecting the learners as subjects of their own learning.

The Learners

An experienced group of community development fieldworkers and managers gathered that first morning in our cow shed. Virtually all of the field staff had university degrees in their respective disciplines: agriculture, nutrition, health, nursing, engineering, community development, management. All had studied in a formal setting in high school and university. Their idea of education came from that formal setting. This training, however, would give them an alternative approach more appropriate for the village settings in which they worked.

They came to these communities as the experts from Katmandu. It was entirely understandable for them to offer solutions to the villagers, to give answers before the questions could be asked, and thus, unwittingly, to treat the villagers as objects of their own professional decisions. These field staff were more than experts in their disciplines, however. They were also sensitive human beings, grass-roots educators whose experience in the field helped them to realize that their solutions often did not work. The water systems they built often went untended. The agricultural advice was often unheeded. Children continued to die as mothers failed to change their traditional maternal practices.

These field staff knew their formal educational practices were not always effective. They had come miles and miles to this hillside, to this *gaiko got*, to discover together a new approach to community education for villagers and teachers who were all subjects. Although they did not entirely understand what popular education meant, they had been willing to trek to this place from their outposts in order to spend two weeks discovering new knowledge, skills, and attitudes. Most of the participants knew some English. We decided early on that whatever we discussed was important enough to be set firmly into Nepali. We had three or four members who could translate from English into Nepali and back. It would slow down the process considerably, but that in itself was a good thing. We Americans were known in Nepal as "the quick ones," apparently wanting to achieve more than is possible or desirable in a given time. But we needed to have the learners themselves set the pace of training. Why? Training is only as good as it is accountable. If at the end of the two weeks I had covered a set of theories and skills, but the participants could not demonstrate their grasp of those ideas and skills, the training would not have been accountable. Considering where we were, on the slopes of the Himalayas, miles from Katmandu, this training had to be one hundred percent accountable. This chance would not soon come again.

It was imperative for me to model, in all aspects of the training, the use of the principles, skills, and attitudes being taught. We had to do what we were teaching. This is a great advantage of such adult education settings. There is neither time nor place for empty words. Paulo Freire of Brazil calls such empty words "Blah, blah." He points out that such verbalism is the result of theory without adequate action. Since translation is precarious at best, we had to make sure that each task being translated could be proven in actions. If the learners did what was being asked, we would know the translation was accurate. Such an arrangement helped me to be very clear and very simple in setting learning tasks. Again, the learners were subjects: they themselves decided what they heard and what they had to do. I too was a subject, in setting the learning tasks, but I was not the only subject in the cow shed.

The ages, educational background and experience of the group were varied. This diversity raised another question: How do we decide which skills, knowledge, and attitudes are appropriate for the entire group? To whom do we aim the training—to the more experienced or to the younger set? In Chapter Three, where we studied the training in Ethiopia during the famine, we examined the skill of needs assessment. Here in Nepal, the breadth of the learning needs made the decision a tough one. I finally decided to present a very basic course aimed at the younger set, inviting the more accomplished to serve as senior partners in the learning.

Villagers proved to be part of the learning community, as well, not only during the practical work but also as they trudged along the path that circled the cow shed. One day, late in the training, as we were analyzing a training design that had been tried the previous evening in the nearby village, an old woman passed by with a great pile of wood strapped to her bent back. She mumbled something as she passed that made the young men chuckle. "What did she say?" I asked. They were still laughing as they translated her disgruntled murmuring: "Talk, talk, talk," she had said. "All they do is talk, and we . . . we learn nothing!"

We stopped our reflection on the training design to reflect humbly on her evaluation of our process. How were we "speaking" to the communities on the hillside who observed our work in the cow shed day after day? What were we communicating to them? The water engineer proposed we take a day from our course to repair the water system that served these villages. We all agreed and spent the next day knee-deep in mud and rocks repairing the walls and platform and resetting the pipes in the mountain so that the water flowed smoothly without interruption. Exhausted, hot, and dirty, and deeply gladdened by our sense of accomplishment, the group gathered for supper at the camp after completing the job.

Some of the participants were concerned that we had lost one day of the workshop. I had to say what was in my heart: "My friends, we did not lose a day from our course. For me, this was one of the most useful learning tasks in the whole workshop! What did today mean to you?"

We heard a fascinating set of responses emphasizing the need to present immediate results to the village communities where they work. One man said, "I learned anew how hard it is to work together." Another, a woman who does health programs, declared that she and her staff were going to do something equally visible and tangible when she returned to her field post. As subjects of their own lives and work, they were applying the day's lesson to the future.

The Program and the Process

Before my arrival in Nepal, the fieldworkers who were to do the training-of-trainers course completed a short survey form:

> By the end of this course:
> 1. I hope to have learned . . .
> 2. I hope to have practiced . . .
> 3. The most critical problem facing villagers in my area is . . .

As we collated these responses, I learned their perspective on the needs of villagers. The problem of women's "ignorance" was mentioned by six participants. Five mentioned lack of awareness and general poverty. Four mentioned lack of trained personnel in the villages and lack of community organization. Three spoke of the need for clean drinking water, for developing local leadership, for learning how to maintain development programs. Many mentioned illiteracy. They wanted to learn how to motivate villagers, how to do program planning, how to get participation in a meeting. They wanted to learn training methods and evaluation methods. They wanted to learn the goals and history of the agency and to discover why it was in Nepal. They asked how to conduct effective meetings and how to maintain programs once they are in place. They wanted to master communication skills, to learn how to do a community analysis, to develop leadership skills and self-reliance in the community.

This was a formidable and sophisticated set of learning needs for a two-week workshop. Indeed, it was a curriculum for a master's-degree course in rural development. The group indicated how keen they were to learn and how well informed they were about the discipline. In light of their responses to the survey, I was able to structure a workshop that reflected their needs. Again, they were subjects—decision makers, along with me—in the content and objectives of this training event. This was an essential aspect of the modeling I promised to do. I demonstrated that it is possible to have a set of objectives for a training, to enter into a dialogue with the learners to check your objectives, and then to amend them as needed. When people see that you are listening, and that they are indeed decision makers with you, their motivation changes dramatically.

On the first day, at our first meeting in the cow shed, we reviewed, in Nepali, a final set of achievement-based objectives. By the end of this two-week session, all participants would have:

- Reviewed current adult learning theory
- Prepared a community map of this area and their own impact area
- Conducted a needs assessment with villagers in this area
- Distinguished between monologue and dialogue
- Examined relationships for development and learning
- Practiced using open questions
- Designed educational events for the villages, using dialogue and the Seven Steps of Planning
- Designed appropriate learning materials

- Prepared achievement-based objectives
- Used all the principles of popular education in their teaching
- Named immediate and long-term indicators for evaluation of learning
- Discovered further learning resources

After they reviewed these achievement-based objectives, we asked:

1. What is missing among these objectives?
2. What is not necessary or irrelevant from your perspective?
3. Which three objectives are most important to you in your job?

Such open questions enabled the small groups to speak honestly, to cite their priorities, and to relax as others named theirs. An open question assumes a variety of perspectives within the group and invites learners to speak as subjects of their own learning. By the end of the morning, we had a set of objectives named by the group as priorities, named by me as basic, and agreed to by all. These were our training objectives. We had set our own agenda as subjects of our own learning. It was quite an achievement, well worth the hours involved.

We learned a great deal about individual perspective in this learning task. I took the opportunity to explain how *perspective* was translated in Swahili as *msimamo*, the place where one stands. Nouns in Swahili belong to classes or categories. This word should have been a place word, *pasimamo*, but in fact it is an m-word, *msimamo*. The m-class words in Swahili are words like person (*mtu*), mountain (*mlima*), river (*mto*), tree (*mti*). These are all places where the spirit lives. We can conclude that the African understood that a person's perspective is a holy place to be honored and respected, even if it is different from another's. Since we are designed to be subjects of our own lives, our personal perspective is vital for us to understand, accept, and honor.

We had demonstrated the difference between "banking" (monologue) and "problem-posing" (dialogue) approaches to community education—as described by Paulo Freire in his *Pedagogy of the Oppressed* (1972)—and they recognized what we had been modeling in this event all along. Freire speaks of "codification of limit situations," showing how a teacher using problem-posing approaches can present the real-life problem to a group through a code—a picture, story, or sociodrama—and then use open questions to "decodify" the problem and offer facts and skills to deal with it (Freire, 1972, p. 103). I have always found such language difficult. There had to be a simpler way to put it. The Nepali staff spontaneously gave us that simpler way: they called these techniques "problem tools." I was delighted to see the Nepali staff take over, as subjects of their own learning, the language of the learning experience—not only by translating the concept into Nepali but also by simplifying the academic jargon into words that worked for them.

A Warm-up for Subjects

We started the program early the first morning in the cow shed by inviting the participants to do a warm-up: to form teams of twos with someone from another post to select a single thing that symbolized their work in Nepal. They had five minutes to find that thing and decide how they would present their symbol to the others.

People presented a shovel, stones, pieces of water pipe, a live chicken, a book, an egg. Each item was seen to represent their work as community education officers. The motley collection symbolized what the agency was trying to do with rural villagers in the mountains of Nepal. Each team was acting as decision maker. No one rejected any symbol. No symbol was better than any other. The design of the task invited equal sharing. There was the inevitable constructive and productive competition as each team wanted its symbol to be a great one. This simply added energy and motivation

to the task. Each team finished in five minutes. Each team presented its symbol briefly and with good humor. No one was left out
as everyone introduced themselves through their symbols. Each
symbol was lavishly affirmed and applauded.

While this can be seen as a simple warm-up activity, it had
more weight than that in the program. It got people working
together who did not know one another well. They came from different outposts scattered throughout the mountains. It got them to
make decisions and use their creative imagination under time pressure. The experience taught them that their ideas were welcome
and would be affirmed. This *gaiko got* was seen to be a safe place.

Durga and his companion selected a hoe as their symbol—
showing how the agricultural programs not only provided nutrition
to families and funds from market produce but were organizing tools
to get farmers to study and work together. The agriculturist organized meetings of men and women farmers to teach new techniques
and distribute improved seeds and fertilizers. As neither Durga nor
his colleague were agriculturists, their symbol encouraged the agricultural specialists among the field staff, since it came from their
peers and colleagues from other disciplines. A major fact in motivation is that advice or praise from a peer carries more weight than
advice, correction, or praise from an outsider or a manager. There is
a certain validity in the estimation of colleagues who know how
hard you have worked to organize a course or do field visits, because
they have done it themselves. The affirmation they heard in the
cow shed became a function of the new culture of this organization. We went on to review the objectives of the workshop and to
show how these aims had been selected from among an infinite
number of possibilities.

In modeling the problem-posing approach of dialogue, we used
a largely inductive design. To teach communication skills, for
example, we first used a simple game: pass the message without
offering a theoretical system for feedback or checking. We set time
limits so the message would surely be garbled before it reached the
end of the line. The message was: "Meet me at the Bissani Hotel

in Gorhka on Thursday, April 25, at 2 PM to trek to Pandrung." The message finally received after a speedy, unsystematic passage from person to person was: "Meet your brother at Katmandu." Everyone had a good laugh at their own expense and recognized that such miscommunication often happens in their work and in their lives.

We then used the Four Open Questions:

1. What do you see happening here?
2. Why do you think it is happening?
3. When it happens in your life, what problems does it cause?
4. What do you think we can do about it?

These questions move from description, to analysis, to application to one's own life, to resolution. They demand that each person act as subject, deciding what the situation means to him and what might resolve it. This is praxis. After deciding that a system of checking was needed as the message was passed, and that writing such a message was the best check, the group passed a second message and it arrived safely, whole and intact. They were quite surprised. This activity offered empirical evidence on the usefulness of checking communications. It was an experience of inductive learning—of praxis.

Groups of three were then invited to design a learning game for the use of village leaders. Many of the groups used music and song in their "problem tools." Once the creative imagination got stimulated in a safe setting where there was no judging—and where working in a team made personal responsibility less burdensome— learners proved themselves creative and productive. This has been my experience all around the world: control the variables and people will produce, content to work hard on their own tasks. What are those variables? They are essentially the principles and practices of popular education, hinged together so you cannot use one without invoking another. The principles that applied here were safety, clarity of task, appropriate time, respect for the product and the producer, and lavish affirmation.

It was hot and dusty in our cow shed. The rain made a mountain of mud on occasion. The working days were long. People were away from their homes and families. These variables could not be controlled. Despite these obstacles, however, learners were motivated—by the safety, the clear tasks, the relevance of knowledge and skills being learned, the respect offered their product when it was shared—to produce their own learning with alacrity and generosity.

A History Lesson for Subjects

The Nepali field staff wanted to know why this organization was in Nepal and what they as staff represented to their village clients and neighbors. How can you use problem posing to teach the history and goals of an agency? Our "problem tool" was a story that they had to complete in teams of three: a description of the beginnings of the agency through the invitation received from the king and queen of Nepal in 1980. Teams had to resolve this problem: Why choose Gorhka district for a work area? How would you select a community for Save the Children to work in? They had in the story a set of criteria for selection of work areas and a list of possible villages. But all the facts were presented as an open system for their consideration. Their opinion as decision makers of the shape of the program in Nepal was invited and respected. Heatedly they debated some of those opinions, and in the debate they clarified their own understanding. They were engaged in learning, and also in creating, the agency's role in Nepal. By their fieldwork they were constantly creating this role in their villages. This theoretical dialogue informed their fieldwork, and their experience informed the theory. It was an exciting dialectic for them to consider.

In all the activities of the workshop, the subject/object distinction was operative. Staff decided whom to instruct in practice teaching, what to teach them, how to design a "problem tool" appropriate for the group, and how to evaluate the learning. Since this group represented only a quarter of the entire field staff of the Nepal field office, it was also necessary for them to prepare to teach their colleagues what they were learning here. Again, by modeling a problem-posing approach throughout, I gave them a basis for the training-of-trainers workshops they would have to conduct when they returned to their own work areas.

Evaluation

Toward the end of the training, on a Sunday afternoon, pairs were sent out to visit families in nearby villages in order to listen for the issues of the villagers: their themes. This is what Durga and his companion reported: "We found a family in a house with a broken smokestack. The owner was angry because the smokestack was not working. We found an old father sick on a bed upstairs. When we visited him we saw that he was taking local medicine. Durga told a story of a friend of his who was very sick and took local medicine and got much worse. When we talked more with the old man, he said he planned to have his son take him to the health clinic to get new medicine."

I was delighted to see how Durga had internalized the problem-posing approach: not scolding the sick old man, but using a story to beguile him with possibilities. How quickly Durga had composed that "problem tool," the story of his friend, at the old man's bedside! It demonstrated Durga's ability with this approach. This was a sound indicator for immediate evaluation of his learning.

During the evaluation session, the staff indicated that the distinction between monologue and dialogue was one of the most useful things they had learned in the workshop. A lovely closure, using music and song, was designed by Rham Bal, a young participant. The lyrics included a chorus of "We sing honor to . . ." and each person in the workshop was named with appropriate lyrics about his or her contribution to the event.

Longitudinal Evaluation

After this training of trainers, participants gave a number of short sessions to their colleagues, so that a problem-posing approach became the educational pattern of this agency field program. Among senior staff there was general agreement that this approach and this philosophy of community development were appropriate for the Nepal situation.

In 1987, one of the participants, K. G. Deepak, a field coordinator in 1985, prepared a significant study demonstrating a way for field staff to work with communities toward turning responsibility for community development over to leaders and members of the local village group. This turnover of control to national and local leadership was recognized as a result of this approach's being used among the staff and in the communities. Only people who have practice in acting as subjects of their own lives can take responsibility for programs and resources and hand over control to others. In 1988, I returned to Nepal to do a "training for turnover" that reinforced basic community development skills and presented an opportunity for a group of field staff to design a comprehensive training of trainers in popular education for the growing staff. (It was at this time that Durga indicated he was confident of his being "subject.")

Reflections

What strikes me now is the development of my own skills through this work. What I know now about doing such a training of trainers is substantially more than what I knew in 1985 at the first Nepal workshop. Who taught me this added knowledge? Durga and company from the mountains of Nepal. Paulo Freire speaks theoretically of the teacher/learner and learner/teacher relationship (Freire, 1972, p. 62). I have experienced this relationship dramatically in my work in different cultures around the world. What is the difference between what I knew when I started my teaching in 1953 and what I now know about teaching and learning? It is a world of difference!

Design Challenges

- Consider your own experience of learning in high school or college, in a professional training program or graduate school. When did you feel entirely a subject of your own learning? When did you make the decisions about what you were to learn and how you were to learn it? If you did not feel like a decision maker in any of these programs, consider what the instructor might have done to make you a subject of that learning. How does this relate to what you are now doing in your teaching programs? How can you use these principles to invite the people who are learning with you to feel they are the decision makers of their own learning?

- What are the political implications of such actions on your part? How will you deal with the new learning/teaching relationships that will evolve if you use these principles? These principles seem so ordinary that it is very easy to say: "I know all this! I have been doing this for years." We have discovered that those who say they know have the least ability to learn. How can we stay open to the potential for growth and creativity—to the kind of transformative change that might occur as we examine these simple intertwined principles and practices of adult learning?

- In your own work, how do you honor the learners as subjects of their own learning?

- What would show you that a group of learners is feeling more confident about themselves as subjects? The surest indicators are behavioral: new ways of acting toward you or toward one another. Do you see these indicators as immediate or longitudinal?

9

Learning with Ideas, Feelings, and Actions

Bloom's classic taxonomy of educational objectives (1956) offers the distinction between cognitive, affective, and psychomotor objectives: ideas, attitudes, skills. The principle we examine in this chapter is the usefulness of making every learning task have an element of all three: ideas, feelings, actions. In this way adult learners will be able to know they know whatever it is they are learning. These elements need not be distinct; they can be, and often are, integrated. When you are teaching a concept, how can you elicit the learners' feelings about the concept? How can you get them to do something with the concept? The more we integrate all three elements, the more critical the learners will be about the concept's significance and the better the concept is integrated into their real lives.

The Problem and the Setting

This integration of ideas, feelings, and actions is the focus of this story of young Mikaeli Okolo, his Zambian colleagues, and his missionary mentors from Europe. Mikaeli is a young Zambian who was educated in theology in Lusaka and in sociology in Rome. He uses his doctorate as parish priest in a small mountain village in northern Zambia. He was a member of a leadership training workshop offered by the Zambian Episcopal Conference to a selected group of Zambian and "expatriate" (foreign) clergy in 1982.

It was with some apprehension that I accepted the invitation from Dick Cremins, a Jesuit priest from the Zambian Episcopal Conference, to work with this group of church leaders on methods of popular education. He called it "leadership training." These men and women had all read Paulo Freire's *Pedagogy of the Oppressed* and wanted to know how to use these exciting ideas in their pastoral work. The very idea of "evangelizing" seemed to stand in stark contradiction to the problem-posing approach, the education of decision-making subjects, suggested by Freire. I took heart from my own apprehension and doubts, however, recognizing that I could not do much "evangelizing" about an educational approach from this personal base of tentative searching. Whenever I start a class or a course, in my own country or in another setting stranger to me, I recall with a smile the myth of a medieval saint who, on arriving at the town walls of a new site for his ministry, got off his dusty old horse and knelt to pray: "Let me do as little harm as possible to the people in this town."

The group had been called from among pastoral leaders throughout Zambia. They had had some training in the Freire-based process of community education, and all had a constituency of Zambian Christians with whom they worked. They had designed some leadership training programs themselves and were using them with their constituents. As they trusted Dick Cremins, they came to work with me on his recommendation. There was little needs assessment done in preparation for this workshop, except for a series of sporadic conversations with Dick. One man was much too small a sample, however, and as a church bureaucrat Dick's perspective was singular. The time frame for preparation was such that I knew I would have to find out about the group during the first days of the six-day session.

The Learners

The group I met at the Zambian retreat house outside Lusaka was as Irish as it was Zambian! A majority of Irish Jesuit priests and brothers, along with a sprinkling of other European nationals who were priests, brothers, or nuns, represented the missionary leadership of the Zambian church. A small number of Zambian priests, brothers, and nuns rounded out the group.

We began, as usual, by telling our personal stories to one another in small groups and then sharing significant aspects of these stories in the larger group. We shared, at the same time, our hopes and fears for this week. Everyone spoke of the hope of learning specific ways to work effectively with their "people," their "parishioners." They wanted practical models for daily work. This much was clear. An undercurrent of feeling was just as clear: on the one hand, they all wanted more clarity of their role; on the other hand, they were all afraid someone would tell them what that role was. Many of the Irish had been professors of the young Zambians when they had been in seminary. These were men and women who had been reared in the absolute hierarchical culture of a religious order and were now working quite independently in rural, distant, isolated "bush" parishes. They clearly felt the tension.

How can one examine the potential of human beings seeing themselves as subjects, decision makers in their own lives, when both culture and a harsh morality put the decision making in another's hands? This was not an abstract problem. On the very first day, evidence arose to demonstrate that this pain was being felt here and now.

The Program and the Process

Discussion, learning tasks, and reading went along on Day One and Day Two as designed. I began, however, to see significant gestures that told me we were not yet addressing their pain. At one point, small groups had prepared some creative material as a model for parish work. As one group began its report, the young Zambian, Mikaeli, got up to describe the group's work. An Irish Jesuit in the same group said to his Irish colleague, "Tom, why don't you give the report? It will be easier for everyone to understand." Tom took the paper from the hands of the startled Zambian, who sat down in shock and shame. No one in the room commented on the incident; nor did anyone oppose what had occurred. Ironically, the subject of the report was equality.

I had to make a quick judgment call. Should I act on this or not? "Not yet," I cautioned myself. "This is too deep. Get more evidence." I was right. The evidence flowed freely. At tea, there was a remarkable self-imposed color bar. At meals, tables were mixed but conversation was not. The men talked to the men; women were often excluded. The Zambians talked to one another; Irish talked to Irish, Dutch to Dutch. The latter even used their own language at times in a mixed group. As presentations were made during the course, the same phenomenon appeared. A woman rarely represented a small group. If we had made a video of the program, the evidence would have been even more cogent. I could not possibly record all the instances of blatant but unconscious ethnocentrism and sexism.

The theme of the workshop, as noted, was "Equality: The People of God as the Church of God." Abstractions flowed from the lips of these men like honey. They were utterly unconscious of the contradiction they were living there and then.

Starpower: A Simulation About Inequality

I knew we had to get out of our heads. We had to bring in the affective and psychomotor elements. But how could we do so in an appropriate mode of action? That was my challenge. The principle I needed was that of meshing the cognitive issue with their affective response and psychomotor activity. I had to respect their roles and their culture, of course, even the hierarchy that was present. I had to trust that they too could be subjects of their own coming to consciousness.

They had all been deeply moved by the political and economic colonialism that Africa had suffered for hundreds of years. The learning simulation Starpower offered a threefold consideration of colonialism: ideas/feelings/actions are called into play as groups are formed in the simulation and then put into an adversarial win/lose challenge. I introduced the simulation as one I had frequently used with great success in having people come to understand the effects of class antagonism. I offered it to them with the caveat that they should test it as learning material and decide in task groups how it could be adapted for use in Zambian rural parishes.

They entered the simulation wholeheartedly. And each discovered, as the simulation is designed to effect, his own tendency to covet a position in the dominant class. Dialogue after the simulation was not so much on how to adapt it as on their sudden realization of their own personal will to power. These men and women could speak their feelings and were honest and courageous. They were all clearly humbled by their experience within that simulation.

That afternoon, as was our practice, we had a celebration of the Catholic Mass. Participants were somewhat subdued as a function of the afternoon's experience, but some spoke of their feelings within the framework of the prayers. At the moment before communion, however, the leader, an Irish priest, inadvertently omitted the traditional kiss of peace. As Carl Jung says, "There are no accidents." The simulated division of the adversarial groups during the afternoon's learning activity was a symbol of the real division among these people, a division so deeply unconscious that no one else seemed to notice the symptoms I saw.

A Daring Simulation

I did not go to supper with them. Instead I designed a daring simulation that would take this bull by the horns. At the end of their meal, I invited them to join me for a unique simulation inspired by Starpower. Everyone joined in. I described the simulated situation and asked them to do some simple learning tasks. "A new government has been elected in Zambia. It is staunchly determined to make all institutions fully Zambian. A law has been passed excluding all church men and women of American and European origin from Zambia. They must leave by the first of next month." I explained that we had a two-part task.

Task A is here and now. All those who will be sent home to the United States or Europe should gather in one group to decide: What will you do in the weeks remaining before you leave? How will you organize for your own personal future? (You can respond to these questions on the personal level.) What are your hopes for the Catholic Church in Zambia? (Offer these as a group.) All those whose origin is Zambian, form one group to decide: What will you personally do in the next few weeks to work for the necessary reorganization of parishes, dioceses, schools, colleges, hospitals, and seminaries of the Zambian Catholic Church? What are your hopes for the future? We will carry on this dialogue in small groups for one hour and then report to the entire group before going to Task B.

Task B is ten years later. You all meet in Rome. What do you think is happening in Zambia? What is happening for all of you who left Zambia ten years ago? Respond in the same small groups: those who have left (Europeans) and those who have stayed (Zambians). We will discuss your speculations in half an hour.

I sat by as an observer, a living video camera, trying to capture the immediate responses. The Zambian group, six men and six women, went at this task with gusto and lots of laughter. Indeed, their energy was so high that one had the fantastic thought that they had been anticipating this opportunity for some time. Their affect was clearly glad and a little bit scared.

The expatriate group, seven men and one woman, was subdued and confused. Their affect was clearly a mix of sad and mad. Voices were dark and murmuring. The one woman in the group kept trying to say something, but she was knitting all the while and sat at the margin of the group. She could not get the men in the group to hear her point. After a quarter of an hour, I went up to the group and pointed out to one Irish priest that Mary Anne was not "in" the group. He was surprised and said: "Oh, I see. Yes, yes, Mary Anne, what is it you want to say?" He had been entirely unconscious of her efforts at physical and verbal inclusion. Here was another symbol of a common lack of awareness.

The Zambian group got louder and louder, with more and more laughter and shouts of "Oh, yes! For sure!" They were working in their own language and the exuberance was felt across the room. The other group became pensive and quiet as the hour came to a close. I asked, "Who wants to share your findings?"

The Zambian group fell silent, waiting for the others to speak. A tall Irishman finally confessed that they were all feeling angry and sad about the law. For many of them, the first concern was how would they sell their cars? (This brought a physical sigh from the Zambian group and, I confess, a shocked expression from me.) Others in the expatriate group said they were all heading to Rome to meet the papal organizers of their respective orders and would wait for the ban to be lifted, which they expected to occur soon. (Another palpable sigh was heard from the Zambians.) The Irish nun said she personally hoped for the best for the new Zambian church and would be cheering for them from wherever her order sent her. The men clearly did not share her optimism but said they were ready to return to help clean things up as soon as possible. My internal video camera was working apace, trying to get as much data as possible for the entire group to consider afterward.

The Zambians all began to talk at once. There was no end to their enthusiasm for this opportunity. There would be no hierarchy, they said. There would be no more building of churches. Seminaries would be closed. Young men interested in ministry would go to work with a priest in a parish to study, using a mentoring system. Women as well as men would run village parishes. Men and women in charge of parishes would work at other jobs to make their living. No funds would be accepted from Rome. Indeed, the Zambian church would send funds to Rome for use in needy situations around the world. Schools and hospitals would be self-sustaining through tuition and fees. There would be an annual conference of all Catholics to decide policy and processes. Zambian forms and symbols would be used in the sacraments.

When an Irish Jesuit interrupted with a sharp "Now hold on there!" a young Zambian priest turned to him with bright, angry eyes and a very sad voice. "When you were my professor in the seminary, didn't you know how you dominated us? Didn't you know how all Zambian forms and symbols were dishonored? Didn't you see how demoralized we were? How could you have been so blind?"

For the first time in my life I saw a priest cry. The Irish Jesuit came over, with great humility and tenderness, sobbing his sorrow and surprise: "Mikaeli, I swear to God, I never realized you felt like this." Soon the whole room was in tears. Simple forms of reconciliation were occurring everywhere, an embrace, a handshake, a rueful shake of the head, a smile. I raised my voice over the crowd and said, daringly, "This afternoon Father John omitted inviting us to the kiss of peace. It seems to me it is time for that now." The affective communication was profound.

After that small ceremony, I invited the two groups to set themselves to Task B. It is ten years later, and you are meeting in Rome. What's happening in Zambia? What's happening for all of you who left Zambia ten years ago? After half an hour, the speculation was exciting. The expatriates had all started working in other parts of Africa with a firm new perspective on their responsibilities to the principles of equality and cultural respect. It was obvious what they had learned. The Zambians shared their projection of hard times and new structures and emphasized their own need to avoid replicating what they had found so offensive in colonialism. They were realistic and more subdued in this projection task, but they nevertheless worked together with alacrity and hopefulness.

Evaluation

It was an exhausted group that left the room that night. The next day, a new tone pervaded the workshop. Tasks went on, lessons about models for transformative leadership were learned and reported, but the process was somehow cleaner, the dialogue more open and honest. When we got to reflecting further on the experience of the night before, a wise young Zambian woman said: "That story and those tasks shook up stuff in me that I never had thought of before! I was surprised how ready I was to think of it!" An old Irish missionary said the same thing: "I discovered how I really felt, what I really thought, who I really was." Mikaeli confided, "I learned what I do not want to be and what I must be as a pastor, as a man."

Over a decade has passed since this educational event. It surely was an occasion of ontological knowing! No doubt the participants in that workshop will remember all that occurred that evening just as well or even better than I am remembering it. The event—affective, cognitive, psychomotor as it was—moved them to know the abstract concepts of equality and mutual respect in startling new ways. Out of different cultural paradigms they responded differently, but with a unity based on no greater ideology than their shared humanity. With new self-respect, these men and women could continue to live and work together.

Design Challenges

Often we use published curriculum materials without amending them to the culture of the group. That culture can be children, African Americans, Hispanics, single mothers, women, churchmen, whatever. As part of our preparation we can examine printed materials in terms of the Who: participants and resource people. Select any printed materials you use in your program. Then consider any single, relatively homogeneous group you work with and examine that material. How will it speak to that group?

Based on this story, imagine a situation and a set of learning tasks you could use with a single group of learners involving affective/cognitive/psychomotor activities. What do you think might happen if you used your design with the group?

Consider anything you teach—a skill (psychomotor), an attitude (affective), a concept (cognitive)—and look at your present teaching plan. Test it for the threefold aspects: actions, feelings, ideas. If you are using only one aspect, how will the design change when you add the other two? One thing we have noticed: when teaching a concept, it is vital to include affective and psychomotor aspects. When teaching a skill, it is important to include the affective and cognitive. When teaching an attitude, we need the cognitive and the psychomotor. They naturally complete one another.

10

Immediacy: Teaching What Is Really Useful

Immediacy of learning is seen in this story as a vital principle that enabled this small group of community development specialists in war-torn El Salvador to grasp what they were learning with both hands. David Rogers, an energetic, thoughtful man, took over management of Save the Children's community development program in El Salvador at a critical moment. Soldiers roamed the streets and the daily news was ominous. Early in 1988, David invited me to conduct a training of the field staff who worked in three or four villages in a mountain area some fifty miles outside the capital city.

The Problem and the Setting

David's purpose for this training-of-trainers course was not only to sharpen the community education skills of the staff doctors, nurses, agriculturists, social workers, and water specialists but also to enable them to take time to examine their responses to the volatile situation in which they worked. As he put it, "I want them to have time to tell their stories, to let one another hear how they are really feeling in the midst of all this."

Throughout the 1980s, El Salvador was a tinderbox. Community development was often used to restore a community after a violent incident had torn it apart physically and spiritually. Government military personnel lived in nervous fear of "guerrillas"; those engaged in the struggle for change lived in fear of the government. I spent a month in Antigua, Guatemala, restoring my dormant Spanish and then took the crowded bus from Antigua to San Salvador, the capital of El Salvador.

At one point after we had crossed the Salvador/Guatemala border, the bus was halted by a ragtag group of soldiers who stormed onto the old vehicle, rattling its floorboards with their boots, their M16 automatics at the ready. My heart stopped when they looked at me and demanded my passport. I handed it to them and held my breath. Visions of what might happen rolled across the screen of my imagination like a dreadful B film with me as heroine and victim. It was a long half hour before they came back, thrust the passport into my hands, and commanded the Guatemalan and Salvadoran passengers, whom they had lined up outside, to board the bus again. As we jolted over the dirt roads into the city, I realized I had just done a large part of the educational needs assessment. This is the kind of crisis the staff with whom I would work were experiencing every day. Little did I realize I would have an even more immediate sense of their struggle before the training was over.

Planning the Planning

The agency has a bright, well-equipped office in a residential district of San Salvador. We spent a week before the training program working together on the plan. My experience with the soldiers on the bus, as well as the daily newspapers and radio announcements of violence, corroborated my passion for immediacy. Since these folks and the people they served were in a daily life-and-death situation, everything we did in the two-week workshop must meet real needs.

David is an experienced Peace Corps trainer, so he and I and the skilled training specialist on his staff, Maria Gonzales, sat together to make our plan. I asked that we first plan the planning. I wanted time in the impact area to meet all the staff and see them at work. I wanted to read all their reports and get to know their reality, so that whatever we taught would have immediate usefulness to them in this critical situation. Then we could, after a few days, sit down with our Seven Steps of Planning to design a draft. I hoped we could have one or two of the field staff to work with us on this design.

Any educator goes into a situation with a boilerplate of concepts, skills, and attitudes he or she wants to teach, can teach. Problem-posing approaches to adult learning do not deny this or judge it as wrong. The operative word is *dialogue*. These people had called me to El Salvador to teach them what I knew. I knew I could not do that with accountability if I did not first find out what they knew, what their life was like, how they thought about it, what they still needed to learn. Much of this dialogue would take place within the two-week training session; some of it had to take place before we even began to plan the session.

There is a strange paradox I have observed: the more structure, the greater chance of spontaneity. I had an experience with a famous psychologist who held a week-long workshop in the Adirondack Mountains in the late 1970s. I attended with great expectations of what I would learn. The first day, however, the 120 participants heard this old man say: "Decide what you want to learn and tell us. As soon as you are ready we shall teach." It was not a happy two days for me before I realized I had to leave. When I told him I was leaving, he admonished me: "Oh, stay! It is so interesting. It will all come out all right." El Salvador in the 1980s was not a research laboratory for innovative learning styles.

The difference between what Paulo Freire calls the "banking system" (where the professor comes and tells you what she knows, so you know it too, with no reference to what you already know or what you need to know) and what Freire calls the "problem-posing approach" (where we work in and through dialogue) is respect for the learners and their immediate needs. It is never an adversarial situation. Problem-posing dialogue is a structured partnership for learning.

Field Visit

Maria and I went off to the impact area. We met the community development specialists, among them Carlos Castillo, the field coordinator who organized community efforts in two separate geographical areas. We saw the two public health doctors and four nurses who were engaged in a huge vaccination program. We met the two agriculturists who worked with farmers and the water specialist who was working with the local government to set up a sanitation system. Local women were secretaries and file clerks in the impact area office and two young men, recent graduates of the local high school, were working as health aides to the public health team.

Carlos and two other field staff were old friends of mine from the international training in Connecticut, so I did not have to start from scratch to build a relationship with them. My struggling Spanish offered opportunities for lots of laughter, and I knew that would indeed be a useful resource. My immediate needs in terms of language, as well as my obvious effort to learn, reversed the roles of teacher and student beautifully. They would be my guides, my teachers, as I rebuilt this elusive skill. In every non–English-speaking country I have worked in, my very desire to learn the language created a relationship with the local people, and my struggling efforts created occasions for hilarity. As we saw in Chapter Five, the power of this relationship between teacher and student is ineffable. Language, even at its most stuttering, can be a help in building that relationship. Maria is fluent in English and served me well as translator. She too was conscious that my faulty Spanish evoked the help of the staff and wisely kept in the background when she could.

Perhaps nowhere else in the world of education is the power of the backseat driver felt as in adult learning. This backseat driver is the quiet kind, a resource who is there to be called on, unobtrusive and safe. Since adults learn by doing, we must design opportunities for this doing, using new knowledge, skills, and attitudes. But *they* have to do it. It is the learners who have the immediate need to practice the skills and attitudes and work with the new concepts. We have to learn to take a backseat gracefully. Just being there is not an easy role for the traditional podium professor. Maria gave me a great example of how to do this well. She would prove herself even more skillful as we developed and led the program.

We visited clinics and schools and farms. We chatted with village leaders and priests and teachers and wives. We played with endless numbers of beautiful, brown-eyed babies, their mothers' eyes shining with pride as I praised each one. Again I saw how basic human courtesy, expressed in respect for each individual and for the cultural practices, is such a profound instrument for learning. I was learning because they respected me. They were learning through my respect. Perhaps, under the umbrella of respect, learning is always mutual.

I did not, of course, write down a word while I was with the staff in the field. Once alone in the hotel room, however, I wrote masses of questions and brought them to David and Maria. It was vital for me, not to understand everything, but to have the right questions. Problem-posing education—in this case in an El Salvadoran mountain village—is a mirror held up to nature, the drama of learning. I have always held that my motto, as teacher, must be: Question the answers! I hope that learners will take up the same attitude. David and Maria were learning too. The more questions I asked, the more they probed their own efforts with the field staff.

I saw the church hall where they proposed to do the training. We had a three-hour meeting of the whole field staff there at which I asked: "What do you wish to happen during this two-week educational event?" I asked them to talk first in arbitrary groups of three, not grouped by the various disciplines like health or agriculture. We asked them if we might audiotape this dialogue so that we could use it for our planning of learning tasks when we went back to San Salvador.

As described in the Ethiopian story, doing a educational needs assessment involves three actions: observe/study/ask. From a staff training session in another national office, the field staff had seen an outline of what we might do during the two weeks. They knew from their three colleagues what we had emphasized in the international staff training in the United States. They also knew that they had a consultative voice here. They were offering suggestions as to what they wanted and needed. It was our role, David's and Maria's and mine, to take these suggestions and decide what we could do in the allotted time, since we had the deliberative voice. Thirty people cannot make such a decision: a plan for staff training. The quality of the dialogue assured them that their suggestions would be honored, and implemented as far as possible, in the name of meeting their immediate needs.

The Program and the Process

The educational event had already begun. There is an immediacy in such an educational needs assessment, in such a visit, in beginning the dialogue. As Arthur Miller's agonized protagonist in *The Death of a Salesman* tells us: "Attention must be paid!" What we were doing in this two-day visit prior to the planning was teaching, using the model that emphasizes listening, respect, dialogue, immediacy, attention to people's experience, engagement, honoring people as subjects their own life and of their own education: all the qualities of popular education.

Happily, David decided that Carlos Castillo, field coordinator, would join us in the four-day planning session in San Salvador. The field staff had expressed their gratitude at having been heard and sent Carlos off with us, knowing the dialogue would continue. The planning process is a central part of an educational event. Maria, David, Carlos, and I worked for four days, using the Seven Steps of Planning, struggling with sequence, setting learning tasks, making materials.

A delightful aspect of this workshop, which has been consistent in every educational event I have been involved in throughout Central America, is the fact that dancing was a given. Indeed, payment of the local band was in the training budget. We would work hard in that training for six days. Each evening the tables and chairs were pushed back, the bandstand was set up, and the room became a fiesta. Here was real immediacy. The field staff appeared not to be tired after a night of dancing—in fact, they worked even harder the next day. Personally, I adore the custom. If there is one educational practice I would insistently urge on readers, it is this one: Dance!

The Seven Steps of Planning

After reading the transcriptions from the audiotape of the meeting with the field staff, the planning group worked out the Seven Steps.

Who. Participants were the two community development specialists who organized efforts in two separate geographical areas, the two public health doctors and four nurses doing a huge vaccination program, the two agriculturists who worked with farmers, the water specialist who was working with the local government to set up a sanitation system, the two local women who were secretaries and file clerks in the impact area office, and the two young men who were working as health aides to the public health team. The entire field staff, along with Maria and David, would be present, sixteen men and women from all parts of El Salvador.

What about other local people with whom they worked closely? These people could not spend six days in such a course. Unless someone was prepared to spend the entire time doing the workshop, they were not included. I call this comprehensive participation. I insisted on it for two reasons: when a new person joins a group, it becomes a new group; and the cultural changes that could be effected by this kind of education would be vitiated by someone not taking part fully in the decision to make such changes. Since David had duties in San Salvador that would involve him on many of the six days of the workshop, he wisely decided not to take part, honoring the principle of comprehensive

participation. As this is a difficult principle to honor when working with very busy people, I often propose making the entire time
shorter in order to welcome people who cannot attend a longer session.

The number of participants is a vital variable for a program's
success. Fifteen was just right for this group. With that number we
could go deep into issues, take time for dialogue, practice skills,
build a bond of new friendship, and make decisions with complete
participation. I was to be facilitator. Maria, who would in fact set
each of the learning tasks, was to be my assistant to honor my
clumsy Spanish and help me in understanding the responses. She
would take part with the field staff in doing the tasks, as well.

Why.   This is the situation that calls for the training event. These
staff people were challenged by a tough professional enterprise:
reaching vast numbers of peasants in their rural impact area with
new skills, knowledge, and attitudes for their own development in
an environment of terror and war. They needed enhanced skills for
this task.

Where.   The immediate issue of safety arose. The agency could
bring the entire field staff into San Salvador and do the training in
a center in the city. Neither I nor the field staff wanted that. They
did not want to leave their families in the immediate danger of that
volatile political situation, and I wanted them close to their work
sites for practical work.

The danger that a gathering such as this training workshop
might be seen by the military as a revolutionary effort had to be
faced. David and Carlos spent long hours with the local soldiers,
explaining our purpose, getting the necessary permits for the event.
This seemed unusual to me, not at all to them. They faced this kind
of minor crisis every day in their work. The immediacy of safety in
the learning situation struck me.

We would work in a church hall adjacent to the agency office.
It had a kitchen so we could make lunch for all the field staff, and

the secretaries could check the office for messages at intervals. The hall was well lighted. It faced a busy street, however, so we had to deal with a variety of youngsters watching events through the open windows, as well as the horrendous street noises of ancient, unmuffled trucks and taxis. Practical work would be done by sector staff in the clinics and on one of the farms where they usually work. The locus of control is related to the site of an educational event. If it is vital to control the number of participants in order to have accountable adult learning, it is essential also to control the place. Imagine the difference if this field staff education had taken place at a hotel meeting room in San Salvador. Consider who was in control in the little mountain town. Who would have been in control in the San Salvador hotel?

Perhaps the principle of immediacy can help us in such decisions. How close to the work site can we get to do the education? This, as we say, is not only for the advantage of practical application but also to ensure that the locus of control is shared by learners. There is a need for a certain physical immediacy in adult learning.

When. We all agreed on six days as the maximum we could ask people to be away from their immediate responsibilities and the minimum in which we could effect the kinds of learning and change needed. The hours of work and meals and dancing were left to Carlos with reference to the needs of field staff to be with their families in the town. I held out for a minimum number of hours together. We agreed that we would work for thirty-six hours: six hours a day for six days. This gave us a framework into which we could design learning tasks.

What For. We then worked to set achievement-based objectives that would enable us to meet the needs and wants of the field staff and be accountable to them. By *accountable* I mean that we do what we say we will do. The structure for accountability involves these objectives (What For) and the learning tasks (How) and, of course, all the other variables we have been describing throughout the book.

In this case, we set up the following achievement-based objectives. By the end of the six days, all fifteen participants will have:

- Described their sector efforts (health, agriculture, and so on)
- Identified some major problems facing them
- Reviewed the current five-year plan
- Examined the situations they have been involved in because of the war
- Reviewed basic adult learning theories for their community education efforts
- Distinguished between monologue and dialogue
- Practiced communication skills
- Designed community education sessions for their sector using dialogue instead of monologue
- Designed problem-posing learning materials: songs, stories, drama, pictures
- Practiced teaching in the impact area using their designs
- Received comments on their designs and their practice teaching
- Celebrated their achievements as field staff in this program

We knew that these objectives would not be the only things done in this six-day event. They simply provide the framework for the learning tasks. As achievement-based objectives, they indicate what the learners are going to accomplish during the allotted time. They are the structure, not the boundaries, of the event. The form of these objectives is significant. They constitute an accountable contract between teacher and learners that promises the learners will have accomplished all this by the end of the course. This form of learning objective is based on research showing how adults learn cognitive, affective, and psychomotor lessons by *doing* them. These objectives demonstrate that the teacher is accountable to the learners and not only the other way around. Accountability is mutual. Achievement-based objectives assure participants that by the end of the session they will know they know. How do they know they know? They just did it.

What.   These were the skills, knowledge, and attitudes that we felt would meet the immediate needs and wants of the field staff. Notice that these skills, knowledge, and attitudes are nouns while the What For (objectives) are verbs. We would learn: the current five-year plan; our recent achievements; how to give and get feedback; basic adult learning theories; the difference between monologue and dialogue; communication skills; situations they have been involved in because of the war; the difference between deliberative and consultative votes; time management skills; how to have an effective meeting. Again, we knew we would be dealing with much more than what was on this list, as we met for six days in that dusty church hall. This was to give us a framework for our efforts: a framework, not a boundary.

How.   This is the program we designed: a set of learning tasks for the group of fifteen field staff. More than anything, I wanted to model problem-posing popular education by avoiding monologue, the accepted norm of educators in Central America. These people had been taught by monologue in school, university, church, and government. By using learning tasks and problem-posing learning materials with immediate usefulness to their jobs in this training session, we might stir in them the desire to use such dialogue in their own teaching.

In all of this, I was aware of the danger of cultural intrusiveness—of insensitivity to time-honored rites and customs. I trusted that I could be a backseat driver who would often have a consultative, not a deliberative, voice in the planning process. Since it was all occurring in Spanish, my linguistic disadvantage was a distinct cultural advantage.

Problem-posing learning is a means to political action: changing the social paradigms. One demonstrates the inadequacies of the old paradigm in an effort to lead people out of it into a new pattern of thinking or doing. This is not easy in one's own culture. How difficult it was to do in another language, another history, another culture, in the midst of war! Political action such as this often takes place on the micro level: a shift of the locus of control when the learner says to herself, "I will decide thus and so." Affirmation of such a decision is one of the major roles of the teacher of adult learners.

The Seven Steps of Planning seem tightly linear as we describe them. If you could have heard the rambling, circular, dancing thoughts and dreams evoked in that little planning group by these questions—Who? Why? What? What For? When? Where? How?—you would see that this structure is itself an opportunity for listening to one another's spontaneity: an opportunity for dialogue. We found these Seven Steps a valid tool to focus the plan on the learners' immediate needs.

On the first day of this training-of-trainers workshop there were no lectures. The learning tasks were all inductive—inviting people to draw from their experiences, to tell their stories, to understand their life and work. When Maria read the summary chart of the research of Malcolm Knowles about adult learning, it was presented as a touchstone against which to measure the factors they had already mentioned from their own analysis. All research was presented as an open system that might be questioned, argued, edited, to apply more immediately to this cultural context. While they were editing, arguing, questioning, they were learning these factors. Later they were invited to describe how they use the prime factor, respect, in their work.

This is what we mean by problem-posing or problem-based learning. Every piece of theory is a hypothesis to be tested again and again in new contexts. This is surely the most scientific of scientific methods. If a theory does not work in a certain context, is it the context that is wrong? The context is real life. In this approach we prefer to look at the theory and see how it can be amended or broadened to apply in a certain cultural context.

An African Anecdote

I walked one June afternoon in 1972 across the broad plateau that forms part of Mount Kilimanjaro in Tanzania. It was snowing! I said to my friends: "But this is equatorial Africa! It can't snow here!" They laughed as we trudged through the snowfall: "That theory doesn't seem to work here!" In the latter half of the nineteenth century a German geologist, Rebbman, sighted the same Mount Kilimanjaro and sent a letter back to his university in Hamburg describing in careful scientific terms the snow-covered mountain near the equator. A departmental meeting was called in Hamburg, and Rebbman's findings were refuted: the committee decreed there was no such thing as a snow-covered mountain in equatorial Africa. The notes of that meeting are still available for perusal, a constant reminder that today's theory is tomorrow's history.

People ask me all the time, "How do you use a problem-posing approach when teaching hard data?" I suggest that you present whatever you are teaching as an open system and invite adult learners to question, to argue, to edit in the light of their own life experience. Thus is theory developed, thus are paradigm shifts catalyzed, thus are adult learners taught as subjects of their own learning. In the design challenges that follow this story, there will be opportunities to design learning tasks using hard data in such a way as to evoke immediate response and learning.

A Dangerous Afternoon

The perils of war-torn El Salvador, which had been described all too poignantly by the staff on the first day of the workshop, were felt by all of us on Day Five. We were quite exhausted, having worked all day and danced long into the night, designed and created learning materials, taught in the field, and worked on feedback. Before starting their second designs, the field staff suggested an outing to the family farm of one of the staff. We packed a picnic lunch and set out to explore Carlos's brother's farm, to walk in the fresh air and take a long lunch break.

Carlos was showing me some of the operations of the farm when his face suddenly blanched in front of me. I turned around to see a great mass of M16 rifles pointing at us all. The soldiers had apparently arisen from behind the piles of hay. There were at least thirty of them, all heavily armed with M16s, grenades, and side pistols. I stood there trembling like a child. One of my best friends, Maura Clarke, a Maryknoll Sister, had died with three colleagues in El Salvador at the hands of military men not many years before. Just the thought of it brought tears to my eyes.

Much discussion in rather loud Spanish got us as far as identifying ourselves as staff of a community development agency. None of us had any official identification with us on this picnic. I was one of the major problems: How did they know I was not an infiltrator? In my dusty slacks and sweater I could have passed for any kind of spy. My trembling did not help much as I lost all touch with whatever Spanish skills I had been so proudly developing through the workshop.

My passport lay safely in my briefcase locked in the office. "For safekeeping," Carlos had said. Right now I wanted safekeeping for all of us, not for the passport. We were corralled toward the road where a radio set was crackling. The young commander of these government troops told us he would check us out with the high command in a neighboring town. It was a harrowing half hour. Later I could look back on it as a great learning experience, feeling what these people felt every day, but at the time I could not appreciate any aspect of it. All I could feel was fear. No abstraction meant anything to me at that point. All that I wanted was the immediacy of a safe conduct back to town. Prayers and deep breathing sustained us during that silent half hour. Where were the dancing, laughing Salvadorans and the humor-loving facilitator? We were learning together how vulnerable and frightened we all really are.

Finally, a thirty-minute eternity later, the radio sparked into life. Gruff voices were heard from afar and the commander turned to wave us into our pickup truck. We drove off in deep silence. No jokes, no laughter, no comments. They knew better than I the dire possibilities of that experience. I thought of Maura and her friends and realized how grateful I was to be alive.

The learning mood of the group deepened after this event. Nothing was said about it. They could not speak about it for safety reasons. The distance between us, however, instead of widening, narrowed. I realized that although I would go back to the United States and relative safety, the moment of vulnerability we shared would never go away. We were bound now by cords of remembered fear and fulfilled hope. The pain of war-torn El Salvador would always be immediate to me. The band came as scheduled that evening, and we danced with a somewhat heightened *joie de vivre*. Some staff from the United States later asked why I did not use that event as a pregnant "code" to analyze their feelings (and mine) about the dangers in which they worked and lived. I was reminded of a phrase I often use when guiding students in the writing of case studies or stories that teach: the materials you use must be close enough to be immediate, distant enough to be safe! Until today, this event has not been distant enough for me to discuss.

Evaluation

Months and years after that six-day training, David Rogers reported examples of the staff's depth and insightful decision making in that impact area. They continued to use the Seven Steps of Planning in their design of training in health, agriculture, and community leadership. We know that political action is rarely the direct result of education. Education can lead to the transformation of those who will then transform the society through political action. El Salvador, like so many war-torn countries, needs men and women strong and sure in their values to effect healthy political transformation.

Design Challenges

- What changes would you propose in the planning design of this El Salvador training-of-trainers workshop if you were involved in it today? Why?

- What else should I have known before starting the workshop? What would have had more immediate usefulness to me and the field staff during that first week?

- Suppose you are designing a training program for managers in communication skills. You want to use the concepts and skills of open and closed communications. How can you present such a theory as an open system, inviting questions, arguments, and editing by the adult learners? What is the advantage to you as teacher—and to them as learners—of doing this kind of problem posing?

- Take any educational event you have designed. Consider what the content is: the skills, knowledge, or attitudes you are teaching. How could you have presented that content as an open system, inviting questions, arguments, editing?

- After all this, what does immediacy mean to you? Why do you consider it vital in designing adult learning events?

11

Assuming New Roles for Dialogue: The Death of the "Professor"

Paulo Freire observes: "Only the student can name the moment of the death of the professor." This story focuses on the clear role of the "professor" and the transformation of that role demanded by this effort at problem-based learning. In the Maryknoll Graduate School of Theology in Westchester County, New York, a group of earnest educators had long been perplexed by the distance between their world of academia and the vibrant reality faced by graduates of their university as they entered their ministry. This reality included not only national but cross-cultural and international situations. Whatever these professors were teaching—scripture, sociology, history, theology, art, physics, political science—needed to be taught in a way that prepared these young people for that complex reality.

The Problem and the Setting

All of these professors had read Freire's *Pedagogy of the Oppressed*, and all wanted to incorporate a problem-based approach into their way of teaching. They simply did not know how to begin. Over the past four years, I had done a short course in popular education with the Maryknoll lay missionaries. These men and women, professionals in law, medicine, nursing, education, and business, responded enthusiastically to the course, which gave them practical methods for teaching in the rural or urban Third World situations to which they were heading.

Professors from this Graduate School of Theology also taught short courses and workshops for the lay folk in this curriculum. After having studied the principles and practices of popular education, however, the lay missionaries became quite critical of the formal methods used by these academics. Why weren't the professors using adult education approaches when teaching their courses? As one professor wisely noted: "We must either study this methodology with Jane or put her course at the end of their curriculum to avoid comparison!"

The Learners

Invitations were sent out to all the professors in the Graduate School of Theology and to all the professors from other universities who taught in the Lay Missionary program. We proposed a three-day workshop to give professors time to reflect upon new research in adult learning, to design a part of their own course using this approach, and to share that design with colleagues for feedback. This would be done at the graduate school in a formal classroom setting. This was their milieu. I wanted to demonstrate how it could come alive and become a place for learning comparable to the abandoned cow shed in Nepal or the church hall in El Salvador. Modeling an approach to learning means being true to it in all circumstances. This was an excellent opportunity to prove that the principles of popular education do not depend on the environment or the operator factor or the topic being taught. Here was a chance to test, under very real circumstances, the entire hypothesis. If it could work with this group of Ph.D.'s, professors, university faculty, in a graduate classroom, it might just be worth further examination.

We actually did this workshop twice for over twenty faculty members from this graduate school and other universities. I was delighted to have Dr. Richard Schaull of Princeton in the group.

He had written the foreword to the 1972 edition of *Pedagogy of the Oppressed*. In that foreword he said: "The development of an educational methodology that facilitates the 'practice of freedom' by which men and women deal critically and creatively with reality and discover how to participate in the transformation of their world will inevitably lead to tension and conflict within our society. But it could also contribute to the formation of a new man and mark the beginning of a new era in Western history."

Richard came to this course with three colleagues from Latin America to discover practical ways to implement the radical theory he had written about in that foreword. There were scholars of many disciplines in the room. There were years of teaching experience. All had at least one Ph.D. and many came bedecked with honors from publishing, research, or teaching. The very fact that they gave their time to this endeavor demonstrated their openness and humility. Deans and administrators joined teaching faculty; men and women, priests and ministers, nuns and mothers. It was a diverse and formidable group.

It struck me that all of these people had gone through graduate school themselves. They had paid all the dues needed to complete their dissertations and to win their teaching and research wings. It was not surprising that they might have internalized the methods of those graduate schools. We teach the way we have been taught. They had all experienced the modeling of traditional, didactic, graduate school methods described by Freire as "banking" and described by me as "monologue." What could a three-day workshop change in their skills and their knowledge, and especially in their attitude toward learning and the learners?

These men and women would certainly be subjects in this learning experience. They would decide what, if anything, of this approach they could use in their graduate courses. We built that choice into the design by inviting them to take one of their courses, use this approach to design a part of it, and then share that design with their colleagues. We began the workshop, modeling a participative, problem-based approach, by inviting their reflection on the objectives and the program. I explained how these objectives had been formed after reading their responses to the question: What do you hope to learn in this three-day workshop? The workshop's aims were stated as achievement-based objectives. By the end of this three-day workshop, all participants will have:

- Reviewed current adult learning theories
- Assessed their own courses for learner engagement and accountability
- Distinguished between banking and problem-based approaches to learning/teaching (monologue and dialogue)
- Used case studies, critical incidents, open questions, charts, found objects, stories, lectures, mnemonic devices, socio-drama, video, seminar and models, web charts, snow cards, and a gallery walk in a problem-based mode
- Designed a section of a course using this problem-based approach
- Designed problem-based learning materials for that course
- Shared their designs with their peers for feedback
- Named future opportunities for studying this approach to graduate education

The Program and the Process

I then showed them the program I had designed to achieve these objectives. The program was a set of learning tasks that they would do together. One of the learning tasks was: "Expectations: Task 2: In groups of three, name your hopes and fears about this three-day workshop." Their responses were significant. A professor of scripture was diffident and concerned: How could he cover the immense amount of material that he had to teach if he used a participative, problem-based method? The ethics professor was skeptical: How can students be invited to make judgments as subjects before they have learned the rules? The political science team, including Richard Schaull, was concerned about equal time for each of their specialties: law, international economics, and sociology. How could they be assured time for teaching all that they had to teach if they used this approach?

Then came their list of hopes and fears for the workshop. They wanted to learn new techniques, learn new methods and practice them, learn how to motivate students to learn, learn how to assure adequate time to cover their material. They asked: How can we be sure learners know what they need to know? How serious is this method? How appropriate for graduate school is this method? How much can we do in a three-day workshop? These hopes and fears are classic. I get very similar ones from field staff in international settings and from social workers and nurses in urban United States community health clinics. With our own experience in graduate school coloring our perceptions, we find it hard to give up the idea that education is merely a sharing of facts and concepts. In the abstract, all these professors knew that effective education involved all three aspects: cognitive/affective/psychomotor. We all are hungry for a sound, empirically based approach to the teaching/learning process that allows us to assure learners that they really know what they came to learn. We call this accountability. We are all terrified, however, at the change in our role such a new approach might demand.

Each learning task in the three-day workshop invited them to practice dialogue with one another and with the resources that went with the task. These resources might be written material, a textbook or an article, a lecture that I offered, a video or a film, an audiotape, a case study. The difference here was that their role as learners was now an active role; they had to do something in small groups with these resources, responding to the open questions that shaped the learning tasks. They began to see the resources as *problem tools*, the name given them by field staff in Nepal (Chapter Eight). They began to recognize that the transformation of their role—from professor (or teller) in the banking approach to co-learner and resource person in this problem-based learning approach—was not as threatening as they had expected.

They discovered that the sequence of learning tasks was of vital importance. We moved from description of a problem to analysis of the causes to application to our own lives and then to an action plan. We used the Four Open Questions to assure that sequence. We used the popular film *Dead Poets Society* with this group and set the Four Open Questions, before they saw the film, to focus their learning. The dialogue among these professors demonstrated the engagement they wanted from their own students. They were clearly learning much from one another.

Evaluation

All of the professors were intense and enthusiastic in their participation in the small-group and large-group work. They were all pleased with the format and the classroom setting, since it corresponded to their normal patterns. All remarked on the obvious need, in this approach, for preparation time. They also were able to cite the personal advantages of taking such time for preparation: the development of their own creativity, their assurance that the process was adequately structured for their own safety, and the development of models for use with other groups.

All indicated fear that they would revert to "banking" or monologue because there was not enough time for planning. The revised course designs they produced during the workshop were clear indicators of their learning. As they discussed these new designs with their colleagues, they often fell back naturally into monologue. Their new skill was to recognize when this occurred. Most had the good grace to laugh at themselves.

Here is a small sample of these designs to demonstrate how quickly and comprehensively these professors internalized the meaning of *problem-based*. Richard's group offered an interdisciplinary module: "Knowing Oppression and Searching Our Resources for Liberation." This had been done as separate modules in the past.

The three professors, however, decided to work together in designing and facilitating a single longer module that would show the integration of all three concepts. They laid out the beginnings of the module, designing learning tasks that demonstrated their concern for safety, for learners as subjects, and for an inductive approach. The most significant aspect of this design was the excitement of the three team members at working together: sociologist, economist, anthropologist. They discovered their own expectations, fears, and resources and, therefore, used these more effectively in their teaching.

The New Testament scholar presented his design: "The Meaning of Ministry." The professor invited small groups, through specific learning tasks, to evoke their own experience with the New Testament. This preparatory activity was designed to motivate learners to demand new insights and the cutting edge of research on familiar texts from the professor as a resource. The professor offered new information in response to questions evoked in the first learning task. In his responses he was creating a dialogue. He had prepared charts and handouts synthesizing and summarizing this new information so he could cover his material. This had been his primary concern at the outset of our three-day workshop. He demonstrated how one can use a problem-based approach, engage the learners, motivate them to think critically, and still teach the established curriculum.

This short workshop experience not only offered these professors a new model for their work. It gave them an opportunity to demonstrate that they had some control of the new model. They worked together to design a problem-based, participative session, led a section of that session with us to demonstrate new teaching skills, received constructive feedback, and therefore had confirmation of their ability to use this approach. How did they know they know? They just did it!

It was clear to all involved that one three-day workshop does not create an educational revolution. Since they were all familiar with the theory through their reading, however, they were able to anticipate further skills development as they practiced this approach. All asked for a second workshop to review their designs and discuss their problems using this approach in their graduate schools. There was one significant problem they all cited: graduate school students expected the "banking" approach. We discussed the obvious need for safety among students and professors and for manifest evidence of the accountability of the curriculum and the teacher. Their own designs showed how cost-effective of learners' time and energy problem-based designs could be. This advantage had to be communicated to resistant learners. We emphasized that participation does not exclude personal responsibility. Working in a small group and working in solitude are two wheels of the cycle of learning. Both are vital to developing not only the concepts, skills, and attitudes being taught but also personal and social skills.

Each of the professors recognized how his role might change when he used a problem-based, participative approach instead of "banking." They named new activities that would be theirs: listening, observing, setting open questions, designing learning tasks, creating synthesis and summary papers that showed the cutting edge of research, facilitating group work, counseling resistant students, setting personal tasks with individual learners. They might, through hard work and study, be able to cite the moment of their own death as professor and their new birth as learner/teacher.

Design Challenges

- If you decide to use some of these intertwined principles of popular education in your own educational programs, how will your accustomed role change? What safety measures can you build into the design to protect your vulnerability in this new role?

- How does the scale of educational programs—the number of students—affect your perception of your own role as professor using a problem-based approach? What can you do to establish a relationship, one that recognizes learners as subjects of their own learning, when you face a class of fifty or sixty students? How can using small groups serve you in such a situation?

- What are the personal signs that you might be reverting to the role of the didactic professor? Who can help you recognize these signs and guide you to a more effective new role?

12

Teamwork: How People Learn Together

Teamwork is a principle of adult learning as well as an effective practice. In this story we will see how this principle worked for Tainie and her comrades in Zimbabwe. This landlocked nation suffered a bloody civil war before whites and blacks teamed up to form a peaceful model of coalition government in Africa. This story shows how learning and teaching teams were used in the education of literacy coordinators in the national literacy campaign of Zimbabwe after independence.

The Problem and the Setting

Tainie Mudondo, one of the literacy coordinators, was a high school student when the call came for Zimbabweans to join Robert Mugabe in 1974 in a guerrilla army that would move the struggle for independence into the forests and mountains. She told me of the day she heard the call. Everyone, she said, every single boy and girl in her high school class, left their books on the desks and went off to the designated center where they began their transformation from high school students to guerrilla soldiers.

Tainie spent seven years in that army. She met her husband there and they had their first child. She went from being a raw, young, frightened recruit to being the education director of the army of liberation. She spent much of her time in the guerrilla army organizing literacy and public health courses for the young soldiers.

After independence in 1981, she was demobilized into a confused Zimbabwean society with her husband and young son. There was a scramble for jobs in the large, modern city of Harare.

A letter from a colleague in Zimbabwe in 1981 brought me the unexpected invitation to become part of the team that would build the new Zimbabwe. This was an invitation I could not refuse. After having spent twenty-three years teaching in Tanzania, during their ongoing struggle for social, political, and economic growth, I was still deeply engaged in Africa. This invitation was from the minister of education, Dzingai Mutumbuku, who had heard through my colleague, Janice McLoughlin, of my work in literacy in Tanzania. Dr. Mutumbuku invited me to join their team to design and implement a national literacy campaign using the army of young men and women recently demobilized from the liberation forces as literacy teachers. I would be expected to train them as trainers of local village youth.

The Ministry of Education was deeply engaged in the thousand and one political problems of the moment. At the bottom of the list lay the issue of the literacy campaign. I was indeed a consultant. While my skills and advice were needed, they would be welcome only when asked for. This had been my role in serving as consultant from the University of Dar es Salaam to the Ministry of Education in Tanzania, so I had good experience in waiting. I learned at this time one of the most useful conceptual distinctions I had ever heard: a consultant has a consultative voice, that is, you can make suggestions; the members of the ministry team have a deliberative voice, that is, they make decisions.

Once I got this distinction clear, I could relax, make my suggestions, and wait. Janice introduced me to Tainie one afternoon in a town square in Harare. Tainie (pronounced "Tiny") is just that: a hundred pounds of intelligent, charming, fun-loving lady with a flair for telling stories and a passionate devotion to her family. I spent much time with Tainie, learning her history in the army and the history of modern Zimbabwe that her story reflected.

The Learners

The ministry knew that their first advertisement for literacy coordinators would bring a flood of applications from former soldiers in the guerrilla army. These young people did not have jobs, nor did they have easy access to places at the colleges or university. It had been less than a year since independence. It would be politically dangerous to invite them to begin a program that was not ready for them. Who decides? This was another critical organizational question for the literacy campaign. Zimbabwe as a developing nation was inspired by reports of the successful Nicaraguan literacy crusade. Zimbabweans wanted to emulate much of what they were reading about that program. But that Central American nation was considerably smaller than the massive landlocked Zimbabwe. A church-based organization, the Adult Literacy Organization of Zimbabwe (ALOZ), had been doing literacy work in Zimbabwe for more than twenty years. Would ALOZ, without a political ideology and with a history of white supervision, be invited to be part of the team? Or would the ministry demand that we start from scratch?

Donald Oliver and K. Waldron Gershman (1989) remind us: reality always includes the observer. I was on the team just by being there, affecting the decisions without making them. My work with Tainie continued as we learned together about literacy and about Zimbabwe, preparing ourselves for the imminent training program. Finally, a decision was made at the upper levels of the Ministry of Education. We would proceed. A team of writers, to which I would be a consultant, would start designing materials for the training workshop for literacy coordinators that would be held in Harare in two months. Materials for the literacy campaign, heavily political, would be prepared by another team and sent to the training team. We would have members from ALOZ on the design team for training. We would not use their literacy materials, however, because they were not deemed politically appropriate for this moment in the history of this young nation.

Before I could teach others how to form a literacy team, I had to learn how to work in one. In this case, my professional soul screamed in frustration at the separation of materials development from training. It seemed to violate every principle of integrated program development. I called on my newfound awareness of my role as consultant with a consultative voice and discovered the joy of detachment. I offered my opinion, gave my suggestions, and waited. This sounds easier than it was. With a strange sort of justice, I was being asked to feel something of what these young people had felt under military discipline for seven years. "Yes, sir; no, sir; no excuse, sir!" Their membership in the guerrilla teams that had eventually won the war for independence had been largely as foot soldiers doing what they were told. This was my role on this design team. I confess it was not easy.

We met regularly under the direction of a young man named by the minister of education to head the task force for designing training. This young fellow also headed the materials development team, so we were linked at that point. Tainie Mudondo was on the ministry's payroll as a teacher assigned to work with the training team to design the training program. She was a vital link to the young men and women we would be teaching, since she was one of them.

Teams Are the Real World

Complicating the political scene at the time (1982) was the fact that the people of the southern part of the new Zimbabwe were not in agreement with those around Harare and in the north. This strong cleft in loyalty and political perspective was reflected in the response to the public announcement about building literacy teams for a national campaign. The people in Bulawayo, central city in the south, insisted that they would not come for a training in Harare. We would have to do two trainings: one for the north in Harare, one for the south in Bulawayo.

In some ways this made our work easier. We would not be dealing with the tensions of a mixed set of political opinions among
the trainees. It meant we had to design two training sessions for
two very different groups. We had only one representative of the
southern group on the training design team. He was a strong man,
a church leader, and struggled courageously to have his voice heard.
If popular education is a way to structure listening and learning,
the making of this training design team was excellent popular education. We had to listen to one another and share leadership. As
an external consultant, I realized how little I knew and understood
of Zimbabwe's history and culture. We had to give leadership roles
to those like Tainie who represented the literacy coordinators we
would be teaching; we had to listen to those representing the
national factions, too, like our friend from Bulawayo.

The teams had to reflect the structure of the rural and urban
society they were addressing. We, on the design team, were not to
decide who would be accepted as literacy coordinators. We knew,
however, that we had to give explicit attention in the training to
the issue of respect for the adult learners to whom these young people would be teaching literacy skills. The pressure of the political
moment precluded the kind of study that would have been most
appropriate for this design team. The report of the Nicaraguan Literacy Crusade indicates how they took that kind of preparatory
time in 1980 before their literacy campaign: "The core team spent
the first month studying—reading about the experiences of other
countries, discussing the small church-sponsored literacy projects
that had been attempted in Nicaragua, talking with experts, writing
position papers, and outlining a possible primer. At the end of Sep-
tember, the core team of seven visited Cuba for a week" (Cardenal
and Miller, 1981, p. 10).

A lesson for all of us is the need for a team to form its own consensus over time, to become a unit with an integrated focus. When
this does not happen, when time is not given to such preparation,
the team usually pays for it throughout the entire program.

A Pedagogy of Shared Responsibility

The slogan used by the Nicaraguan Literacy Crusade in their orientation program to train the immense teacher corps of high school and college students in the 1981 Nicaraguan program was "A Pedagogy of Shared Responsibility." We in Zimbabwe used their experience as a framework for designing the training of literacy coordinators. In Nicaragua,

> The teacher's manual provided step-by-step instruction on the use of the literacy methodology and also contained detailed back-up readings for each of the twenty-three themes. It gave the *brigadistas* the necessary social, political and economic information to generate a knowledgeable discussion and dialogue. Since the Crusade was considered a reciprocal learning process, the handbook also outlined a systematic set of study activities for the volunteers. The basis of their learning was their own living and teaching experience. As such, they were responsible for conducting a careful research study of their communities and keeping a field diary of their activities [Cardenal and Miller, 1981, p. 19].

There were significant differences between the Zimbabwean and Nicaraguan campaigns. Zimbabwe's literacy coordinators would be paid staff of the Ministry of Education, and this campaign would be an ongoing service of the ministry. The design I proposed for the training of literacy coordinators incorporated some of the reciprocity issues named by the Nicaraguan crusade. The coordinators would be learners as well as teachers. If we were to do this training well, it would not only be Zimbabwe's preliterate men and women who would benefit, but the coordinators themselves.

The Program and the Process

We made work teams the basis of the entire experience. Remember, these young people had very recently been on military teams, driving a tank together, or flying a fighter plane. They had seven years' experience of military teamwork. How was this to be similar for them? How would it be different? My concern in the design was for modeling—demonstrating the kind of respect and listening that we all knew was essential if these young people were to reach the hearts of their elders whom they would be teaching how to read and write. I could bring technical expertise, and I did. I could bring planning skills and design skills and evaluation skills, and I did. But I knew all too well that these skills were not the heart of the matter. The heart of the matter lay in the meaning and potential of the dialogue that would have to occur among team members and between literacy coordinators and the adult student. Their first job was to learn to listen to one another in their own team and show respect to one another in new and appropriate ways. On the first day of training, we invited each team to decide together on a team name related to the recent war of liberation. Many chose names of fallen comrades from the struggle. They were deeply moved as they introduced themselves and their teams by these honored names.

Using a strong element in African culture, we invited teams to create or share songs they could use in teaching. Early on, in the first training, a group of six men and women began to sing the marching song they had sung as guerrilla soldiers: "The Soldier's Song." It was a beautiful moment, and the whole group took it up quite spontaneously. At that moment of the training workshop, the difficulties they had experienced getting selected for this job, the confusion and ambiguity about their role, all fell aside and they found themselves back in the unity of purpose of a team that had won the war of liberation. These two team tasks, naming their teams and selecting a song, had achieved what was needed to get us started with the training in how to teach and how to use the Zimbabwean literacy materials. They had worked as a team, made decisions with some consensus, watched leadership emerge among themselves. There were no lieutenants and captains now, no stripes or rank. Team leadership would emerge by action.

When setting team tasks using open questions, it is important to realize that the trainer does not know the answer to the question. The facilitator has no control over what the team will say or how it will respond. We found that the leadership of one team's sharing "The Soldiers' Song" evoked a great deal of energy in the other teams to do as well or better. This is the element of *com + petition* that such teamwork offers. These young men and women were challenging one another, asking how far they could go together. The Nicaraguan training used a Central American genre called the couplet, a popular literary expression. In Zimbabwe, we used the *methali* or proverb to summarize or question what we were learning. Each team selected a familiar proverb, or made one up, at the end of each day to synthesize all that they had learned about teaching literacy that day. "One hand does not wash itself!" "On the third day the guest receives a hoe!" Such proverbs caught the wisdom of the language and the people.

It was not hard to find preliterate adults for practice teaching classes in Harare where we did the first training course. We happened to be at the University of Zimbabwe and were able to enroll a small group of physical plant staff as learners in the first round of the program. The teams decided who would teach, and how they would arrange the situation, so that they could both observe their colleague and also respect the learner. Each team selected a set of evaluation indicators that was then reviewed by the entire group. They held their friend's feet to the fire with those indicators. We did some work beforehand on how to give and get feedback, so that there would be no defensiveness and no attacks. The practice teaching sessions were an excellent chance to test the written materials, as well. As these were still in draft form, the young people knew their recommendations would be given serious attention. I would like to have had a video camera at the practice teaching sessions. The films could have been reviewed by the entire group, and the learning would have been shared by all. When we use video, the learning is immediate and affective and the data are objective.

Evaluation

Immediate evaluation—measuring how well they know they know—told us that all the young people, in both sites, north and south, could demonstrate the skills they needed to design and teach literacy. Their practice teaching sessions were personally reward-ing to themselves and to the adult students. They felt, and demon-strated, a bond to their team members.

Long-term evaluation, the effect of this training session on their future work as team members of the ministry managing the literacy campaign, was less encouraging. We had designed a careful sequence of tasks in the six-day training workshop, but there was not a care-ful sequence of follow-up work with the teams of literacy coordina-tors after they started their job. The team structure, used so well in the training sessions, was not utilized for follow-up and support of the literacy coordinators in their widespread teaching posts around the country. Tainie was not in a position of power at the ministry to get systems for follow-up and support of the teams of literacy teach-ers in the field. If they had maintained the team structure, even with teams of two, and nurtured those roles and relationships, they could have created a long-lasting program. The ministry needed a cur-riculum of ongoing training for these young people.

The teamwork aspects of this training program were sound. There is no way these men and women could have learned what they learned in six days without having done so in those working teams. Team tasks were sometimes completed without any inter-vention from trainers. Tainie worked as a team member, and I was out of the loop because they often worked in their own language, not in English. Their learning in their teams was both autonomous and independent. Such autonomy and independence is the pur-pose of a literacy campaign. The people of Zimbabwe did not sim-ply need to learn to read and write; they needed to learn to work together as members of village and community teams, to create a new Zimbabwe.

Design Challenges

- We often invite people to work in small groups. Having read this account of the teamwork efforts in Zimbabwe, as well as the story in Chapter Eight on teamwork in Nepal, can you see that such an invitation is a challenge to a new way of working and thinking? What happens in the small groups is not vicarious: it is real life! There is no "getting back to reality" but, rather, a getting *down* to reality in doing a learning task as a team. This puts the burden on us to compose teams wisely and well. Teams may be composed by the adult learners themselves; they may be composed of homogeneous or heterogeneous folks by the teacher; they may be composed by chance. In any case, the composition is intentional. And it is your responsibility. What have you learned here about composing teams in your next training event?

- A learning task done by a team involves peer pressure and many overt and hidden dynamics within the group. How much of this can you command? As you saw in this example from Zimbabwe, none. The team is a group of adults, and the responsibility to learn is theirs. Your responsibility is to compose teams and prepare a well-formed educational design. You cannot learn for others. The team (or small group) is there to help one another learn. Your detachment is of value to yourself and to the adult learners. Trust the team! Consider a time when you, as teacher, wanted to interfere in a team or small-group activity. What was the advantage to you—and to them—of resisting that temptation?

13

Engagement: Learning as an Active Process

This is a story of the power of engagement as a principle of adult learning—a principle that enables learners not only to take part in learning but also to practice learning as subjects of their own lives. In this case the learners took an active role in the design and structure of their own future in an organization.

The Problem and the Setting

Hospice as a health care movement has been growing like the proverbial Topsy. There is an immense need for the loving care of hospice nurses, social workers, chaplains, volunteers, and aides who come to the homes of the sick to serve not only the patient but also the families of those who have been diagnosed with limited life expectancy. The growing threat of AIDS has made the growth of hospice care even more critical.

In eastern North Carolina, a large hospice found itself growing even larger, as more and more families applied for service. The communities were getting more and more involved, and so the volunteer cadre was increasing. The funding base was constantly strained and the need for more resources—personnel, finances, structures—was obvious. The executive director, a caring nurse and an astute administrator, realized it was time to learn and do some strategic planning. As she said, very wisely, "We must all learn to think strategically. This growth will continue!" She was determined to make this planning process fully participative, engaging as many staff and board and community members as possible. She called Jubilee and invited us to design and lead the program. How could we use the principles and practices of popular education to engage the entire hospice community in planning for their future? How could we use the principle of engagement in the earliest planning steps?

The Learners

This hospice community was a model of diversity: nurses, administrators, physicians, accountants, aides, chaplains, social workers, volunteers. Some had been with this hospice since its beginning in the early 1980s; others were newcomers. Some had graduate degrees; others were graduates of primary school. We made it clear from the beginning that everyone involved did not have the same role. The policy and program priorities that evolved through this strategic plan were a decision of the hospice's management team, which is composed of department directors: nursing, volunteer services, administration, and so on. Once these priorities were set, the board of directors had to approve them in light of the budget.

Ultimately the executive director had the deliberative voice—that is, she made the decisions. She gratefully shared this voice with the management team. All others, throughout the planning session, had a consultative voice—that is, they made suggestions. Once this distinction was made clear, the process could work smoothly. All would be engaged; some would make the final decisions. If this distinction is not made, participants who are engaged in naming priority issues and program innovations may expect their pronouncements to become policy. The distinction clarifies each person's role and invites creative suggestions.

The Program and the Process

The principles and practices of popular education worked here to bring many people together in a planning process that actually led to a feasible three-year plan. We at Jubilee first studied all the documents we could lay our hands on dealing with the history of this hospice. We studied the demographics and were shocked at the size of the growth. We spoke with a sample of staff and board members to get a sense of the mood and the status of the program as well as the organizational development. Their engagement with us in this data gathering gave us a sense of the diversity of perspectives at work. Through the community survey, we were able to hear from a wide sample of the community as well.

The community survey form was given to each staff person, who was then asked to select one person in the community whose opinion they valued. There were three questions:

1. What has been your personal experience of hospice?
2. What one thing in hospice do you value most?
3. What one thing would you like hospice to do that we are not doing?

We had a 70 percent return of these surveys and presented all the raw data to the staff to use during their one-day workshop. It was the means of engaging the community in this strategic planning and demonstrating to the staff that they were the vital link between the hospice and the community. Selecting the person they surveyed was practice in autonomy, demonstrating that they were indeed subjects of this process. The voice of the community was heard also through the board members and through the cadre of volunteers.

We used the basic outline for strategic planning from John Bryson's *Strategic Planning for Public and Nonprofit Organizations* (1988) and the Seven Steps of Planning to set out a draft program to engage all three groups of participants: staff, board, and management team. Bryson gives a sequence of concepts: stakeholders, mission, SWOT (strengths, weaknesses, opportunities, threats), strategic issues, strategies, action plan. We used the Seven Steps of Planning—Who, Why, When, What For, What, Where, How—

to design appropriate tasks that would engage all participants in responding to these strategic planning steps.

In terms of the time frame—the When in the Seven Steps—we arranged for three different sets of participants (the Who). First we worked with all the staff. All seventy-six staff members, including the management team, came freely to the one-day workshop. Three staff members interrupted their vacations to attend. They wanted to be heard in the design of this strategic plan. We had a second one-day workshop with the board of directors and management team, and finally we had a day-long workshop with the management team, which tied it all together and prepared a plan for the board to review.

Here is how we used a learning task to define strengths, weaknesses, opportunities, threats:

- What For: Prepare a SWOT analysis: internal strengths and weaknesses; external opportunities and threats.
- How: Task A: At your tables of four, identify all the strengths of hospice and write them on the chart on your table. We'll hear a sample and record them all. Task B: Identify all the weaknesses you perceive in hospice. Task C: Name the opportunities you see facing hospice. Task D: Name the threats you see facing hospice.
- Materials: Each table had a chart on which to record their work. These all went into the report, which was used by the participants in the next session.

The immediate relation of content, objective, and task drew all groups into intense engagement, especially because the time frame was so short. We have discovered that the shorter the time frame for a task, the higher the energy.

The aims of the workshops were set out as achievement-based objectives. By the end of this day, we all will have:

- Named symbols of our work in hospice
- Identified stakeholders in hospice by using data from each hospice's community survey
- Edited the new mission statement
- Prepared a SWOT analysis: internal strengths and weaknesses; external opportunities and threats
- Identified strategic issues in this hospice today and selected one from each table cluster
- Named one practical alternative that would address this issue
- Identified the barriers to this practical alternative
- Prepared a proposal for implementation

These objectives were achieved in a six-hour period by seventy-six staff and four board members by having them do small-group tasks at tables of four. This arrangement assured comprehensive engagement. Even the most reticent staff person could raise her voice in such a setting. As we gathered data from all the tables, we noticed a growing consensus of attitude and opinion. We also heard dissenting voices that were honored. The report of this six-hour meeting, recording the tasks that completed the nine objectives, was thirty-six pages long. This was the data base offered to the board before they began their similar workshop.

The comprehensive engagement of all staff members was informed by the response of community members to the survey. This staff report in turn informed the work of the board of directors, who enhanced the data base for the strategic plan through their suggestions. They added their perceptions to those of the staff and proceeded to name priority issues for action. Finally, the management team faced this mass of data and distilled it into a specific set of action plans that they presented to the full meeting of the board of directors. That is indeed engagement.

Evaluation

Immediate evaluation of the learning and progress toward a viable strategic plan indicated that all participants were surprised at how well they had achieved the nine objectives. The design of the program, based on all the principles and practices of popular education, assured that outcome because it was accountable. People were in small groups, mixed as to their role in hospice, and worked as teams to achieve the objectives. Team reports were enhanced by the individual voices that were raised to say: "My team said this, but I feel differently." This was an indication of the safety they felt in the room.

Here the educational objectives were also production objectives because they were generating data for future use. We, as facilitators, shifted the tasks to fit the time so that the six hours were fruitful. There was incredible energy in the room. Since all participants were there of their own volition—as subjects of this operation—they were vigorous in their honesty and effort. Their engagement was at once the means to an end of producing the strategic plan and also an end of the design that used the principles and practices of popular education to get them fully engaged. The operative question for short-term evaluation of a popular education function like this is, "How do they know they know?" In this case, all who were engaged in this process celebrate their engagement by the fact that their suggestions are visible in the agency's priorities. At the very least, their suggestions were in the data base of the plan. How do they know they know strategic thinking and planning? They just did it.

The chaplain and president of the board of directors both made the same comment to the director about the process: "These folks are tough!" They meant we had a design that would not let participants stray from the purpose. The design, and our relentless implementation of it, demanded intense engagement.

What about the long-term indicators? Not only is a strategic plan in place for this hospice team and community, but action is under way on a number of fronts. They have a Gantt chart (calendar) that is used daily to measure their progress, as well as a common language that all can use to identify and change priorities. Long-term indicators are sometimes seen as impact evaluation. The results of a planning process like this in a large community agency are not only having an effective plan in place but also having a plan at work in the agency, in the community, in the homes of patients. The question we use to do long-range evaluation of community education is: "So what?" After three months, there are strong indicators that the focus of this hospice is clear and priorities are in place.

Design Challenges

- What are some of the indicators you now use in your educational programs to show that adult learners are fully engaged?
- What is the advantage to you as teacher when adult learners are engaged, working in small groups or teams, completing learning tasks, raising their voices with suggestions or even protests about your program?
- What is the advantage to the agency's management team of having so many people engaged in the preparation of a strategic plan?

14

Accountability: Success Is in the Eyes of the Learner

Accountability of adult educators to their learners is a startling principle, especially when those educators are physicians. At the world-famous International Center for Diarrheal Disease Control (ICDDC) in Dacca, Bangladesh, a small group of physicians invited me in 1986 to teach them the principles and practices of popular education during a single week of training. I have worked with teaching physicians at the University of North Carolina Medical School and with young interns at Duke Medical School, as well as with doctors in Save the Children programs and physicians from the Pontifical Catholic University in Chile. Few of these doctors had ever before examined their teaching approach.

The Problem and the Setting

In the ICDDC, the task of teaching patients how to prevent diarrheal disease was a vital part of the curative and preventative program. This was a referral hospital receiving those cases that could not be handled at the local level throughout Bangladesh. For these patients, who arrived close to death and left the hospital with a new lease on life, this was the teachable moment. The family crisis around their coming to Dacca and staying at the hospital certainly got the attention of their local community. Indeed, they were the patient celebrities of their villages.

What doctors knew as teaching methods—telling these recovering patients how to prevent a recurrence of this horrible situation for themselves or for other members of their family—was simply not working. The staff saw patients come in again and again. Or they saw other members of the same family arrive, drawn and dehydrated, as near death as any human being can be. The spoken message was simply not getting through.

Public health campaigns on the issue of diarrheal disease control have proliferated in Bangladesh. Although this training of a small number of doctors in popular education was not a major component of the national campaign, if a few physicians began to consider alternative ways to teach these adults, a new beginning could be made. We all understood this, and the doctors were pragmatic, practical men and women. They gave their time to this venture because they hoped it could literally make a difference.

The Learners

Assura Lori is a middle-aged grandmother, a bustling dynamic woman who raised a family of four sons and has her own medical practice, working in clinics and hospitals and continually doing research on the number one killer in Bangladesh: diarrheal disease. She holds a professor's chair at the University in Dacca, and works tirelessly at ICDDC to cure and try to prevent such disease. It was she who heard about the community education efforts of Save the Children and contacted a Washington-based funding source to explore a training program for doctors at this hospital. The funds came through and I headed to Dacca with virtually no information about the physicians with whom I would be working. I knew only that they would be doctors on the staff of ICDDC and, therefore, men and women of long experience. They would be middle-aged or older. My gray hair and long years of experience in Africa, Asia, and Latin America would at least get their attention! I needed to know a great deal more about the group, about how they taught, about their problems in the hospital, and about their personal achievements. This needs assessment was going to be tough, and very necessary.

Even for my travel-worn eyes, Dacca was a shock. Not since Calcutta had I seen so many people in one place at one time and such evident, gnawing poverty and hunger. I met Dr. Lori at her office in the hospital the first day, and she wisely gave me some things to read and sent me off to sleep for the day. "Otherwise," she smiled, "we shall be dealing with your jet lag for the whole time!" I thought: sleep can deal with physical jet lag; nothing can deal with the cultural jet lag experienced by a well-fed American arriving in Dacca, Bangladesh, visiting the Hospital for the Control of Diarrheal Disease. I felt once again the overwhelming humility I had felt in Mali, Ethiopia, Tanzania, Kenya, El Salvador—everywhere I had come to teach and stayed to learn. While such humility in the face of the complexities of an unfamiliar culture may be healthy, it is not a very pleasant feeling, for it comes mixed generously with rank fear: What in the world am I doing here? How dare I teach these people?

Sleep did help. The gnawing fear never went away, however, and I believe it is well that I felt it. Carl Jung (1969, p. 4) teaches: "Whoever reflects upon himself meets the frontiers of the unconscious, which holds all he needs to know." I would soon find that my honesty in dealing with this fear would be brought into play again and again as I worked to teach these physicians the principles and practices of popular education.

I spent two days at the hospital, at the bedside of frail and withered men, women, and children suffering from diarrheal disease, interviewing the doctors who would take the course, talking to nurses and aides about their work. These were the true patient educators, more effective than all the doctors. We had to begin at the top. This was a political decision in which I played no part. The hope was that these doctors would teach the nurses and aides what they had learned. I knew this would not happen in any formal way. Physicians do not have that kind of time. I realized there and then how vital it is to be in a position to select the participants in such a course for optimal replication of skills and knowledge. One does what one can at the time, trusting that the seeds will bear fruit the sower will never see.

Dr. Lori invited me to her clinic in the city where she saw patients before sending them to ICDDC. I saw families dealing with this overwhelming and endemic reality with quiet submission. These were the adult learners the doctors faced every day. How would the principles of adult learning help them in this demanding situation?

Bangladesh itself has been a wellspring of research on popular education. The country lends itself, with its vast numbers of rural and urban illiterate needing to know so much to cope in a new industrial society, to such an approach. Indeed, popular education centers throughout the country have produced excellent materials on literacy, agriculture, health, and management of small industries. I realized that these centers could be valuable resources for follow-up on the skills, knowledge, and attitudes learned this week by the small cadre of doctors. In my preparation for the week, I visited one of the education centers near Dacca. As political issues kept these centers from serving the medical profession as much as they would like, they were very supportive of my effort, minuscule as it was in the face of their national problems. They offered me all the materials they had developed on the issue of health and graciously offered to serve as a referral after the course.

Dr. Lori and I spent three days hammering out a program that would be relevant and immediate for these physicians. I realized at once that the participant physicians could not be present for all the sessions, since the course would take place at the hospital and they would be on call for emergencies with their patients. Regular hospital meetings had to be attended throughout the week, as well. We found ourselves planning a course in the interstices of their days. This phenomenon is one I have met in virtually all of the forty-eight countries where I have worked as an educator. The fact is: education is not a priority. There is nothing we can do about this attitude directly. We must simply face it and name it. The wisdom of Swahili has a proverb: *Ubora hauhitaji sifa* (Excellence needs no praise). Our task as educators is to make the learning so accountable, the engagement so meaningful, the immediacy so useful, that this unhealthy attitude will change in time. As long as education continues to suffer from narration sickness (Freire, 1972) and is not accountable and engaging and immediate, as long as it continues to be what Donald Oliver and K. Waldron Gershman (1989) call "miseducation," such a lack of respect will continue.

The Program and the Process

Dr. Lori and I set to, with the time available to us, in the place available to us. My fear and trepidation rose as we worked out the Seven Steps of Planning for the course.

Who.   Twelve physicians from the ICDDC, eight men and four women, all with long experience in medicine, had volunteered to take this course.

Why.   ICDDC is a teaching hospital not only for the university medical school but also for the patients and their families. The formal education methods these doctors know from their own experience in medical school and professional training do not work with unlettered (often preliterate) Bangladeshi citizens who come to this hospital. The doctors, as I watched them with their patients and the other health professionals, were comfortable talking about the situation as an abstract problem. They stayed, during an educational session with desperately sick patients and their families, in their heads. These doctors—indeed, all the staff of ICDDC—needed a process of popular education that would be accountable to patients and their families, so that these people would know they knew when they left the hospital.

When.   I insisted we should organize the course so that all participants attended all learning sessions. In light of the inevitable emergency calls and regular hospital meetings, that gave us the possibility of four hours a day. This decision—not to have people coming in and out of the course—emerged from my experience that when one person enters or leaves a group, it becomes a new group. The intensity of training in popular education, the fact that learning tasks are done in small groups, the fact that bonding takes place among learners—all justified this decision to work in a shorter time frame with all twelve participants. It was also an opportunity to model with the physicians the principles of respect and inclusion that we were in fact teaching them to use when they would be training other health care personnel in this approach. Four hours for six days gave us the modest total of twenty-four hours with the group. It was a challenge to select the most useful learning tasks for this time frame.

Where. There was no way these physicians could leave the hospital for a week. Their responsibilities kept them close to patients and colleagues. So the course had to take place at the hospital in a dark, windowless meeting room with a rusty old air conditioner filling the space with a steady noise and cold blasts of recycled air. This meeting room had one large old table that filled the central space. It was designed for a hierarchy: the teacher at the head of the table and doctors ranked by status around it. This was the room in which staff development sessions took place, as well, so their memories of other events in the room would be competing with our approach. Our challenge was to structure small-group sessions around that table in ways that could work for the doctors.

What For. Dr. Lori and all the physicians had been given copies of my book *Learning to Teach* and were frankly not impressed by the simplicity of the approach. Dr. Lori and I struggled to design immediate, engaging objectives that would challenge this sophisticated group of professional men and women. She was admittedly frightened by the simplicity of the tasks in the book. These people, of course, were used to dealing with complex quantitative data and reading journal articles replete with specialized language. Although I was tempted to couch the principles and practices of popular education in such jargon that they would spend the whole week deciphering, I overcame the temptation and held my ground. Popular education is a complex and subtle technical art form. There is no need to codify that complexity and subtlety in esoteric language or masses of quantitative data. I told her that I was offering them an alternative from the real world. If they wanted to explore it, we would do so in simple terms and clear learning tasks. The principles and practices of popular education are expressed in popular language. If they wanted esoteric language and studied complexity, they had the wrong teacher.

At this point, I recognized I could not compromise without losing the whole purpose of the project. I was there with what I knew of popular education. It might or might not work in ICDDC, but we had to try it—not some rarefied version of it designed to fit into what was clearly an unhealthy mold. This moment felt not unlike the moment in Ethiopia when Fatuma and her rifle saved my day. Where was Fatuma when I needed her in Bangladesh? Dr. Lori took a deep breath and admitted: "You are right. If it does not help us teach these people what they need to know to survive, we must decide that later. Right now, this week, you must teach us as you know best." I assured her that her decision would at least give us a chance to model popular education with the doctors.

This is one of the most compelling aspects of popular education. You must use the principles and practices to teach them—or else you do not teach them. It is as simple as that. To use the banking approach, to talk about popular education as if it were an abstraction, is not only not to teach it: it is teaching, through that modeling, the banking approach. In this business, we are always hoist on our own petard.

So we accepted some basic achievement-based objectives for the doctors. By the end of these six days (twenty-four hours), we all will have:

- Identified the educational problems of ICDDC
- Shared stories of successful learning events with preliterate learners
- Reviewed adult learning theories
- Designed open questions and practiced using them

- Completed a thematic analysis of a sample of patients, discovering their themes or issues that move them
- Distinguished affective, cognitive, and psychomotor aspects of learning (feelings, ideas, actions)
- Identified familiar communication modes of Bangladeshi families
- Reviewed and adapted useful theories of communication
- Examined cultural possibilities for communication in song, drama, dance, film, video, radio
- Examined the difference between monologue and dialogue
- Designed materials for preliterate and literate patients and families using the Seven Steps of Planning and dialogue
- Designed a set of learning tasks using these materials
- Evaluated this course daily and made course corrections for greater immediacy and engagement and ultimate accountability

What. The content of the course—the skills, knowledge, and attitudes they would learn—would be the principles and practices of popular education; the affective, cognitive, and psychomotor aspects of learning; theories of communication; design and use of open questions; themes of learners; communication modes (direct, indirect); the difference between monologue and dialogue; the learner as subject (never object); design of learning tasks; design of learning materials using dialogue; and evaluation indicators (immediate and long-term).

How. The physicians would learn popular education by doing it. I wanted to be sure we gave these twelve doctors a real taste of popular education, so the learning tasks were somewhat more radical than usual. Having seen them in action with their patients and staff (even though I did not understand the language), I knew we had to give them a chance to get out of their heads and into their hands and hearts. I insisted also on a video of the program from beginning to end. This would give us a chance at replication, a document for the funding group, and a useful monitor to make sure the doctors were there for all twenty-four hours. We used the video for feedback and evaluation, as well, during the course. The funding organization sending me to Bangladesh agreed to provide resources for hiring a professional video technician and equipment and processing. I would urge all educators to ensure this is in the budget for every educational program.

Evaluation

Daily formative evaluations offered us more and more input on the overall design of the course so we could make it more and more immediate for the physicians. The open questions of the force-field evaluation process—What was most useful for you today? What shall we change tomorrow?—gave them emotional freedom to object to tasks that seemed culturally inappropriate, and to demand tasks more immediate to their needs. Because of the need for immediacy in this process, we accepted most of their changes. By now, they had the deliberative voice in the course. They themselves asked for more hours, and we ended having six hours on the last two days.

For long-term evaluation we put them in touch with the director of the Bangladesh Research and Action Center (BRAC), where they could get materials and further instruction in popular education. There were no systems in place, however, to reward such efforts, nor was there ongoing funding. Today I am convinced that single events such as this course in Bangladesh are somewhat futile. They might make a difference in the approach of one or more doctors. But without organized follow-up and systems for rewarding new learning and revised efforts, the burden on the individual is too great to be sustained. I often say there are three things that make accountable learning happen, and they are important in this order: time, time, and time. Without reinforcement, without a sequence of continued learning activities and a research agenda, without the stimulation of appropriate rewards and motivation, professionals will go back to teaching the way they were taught.

The enthusiasm of these twelve doctors and their animated engagement during the short course were perhaps a function of my involvement with them. What do they need to sustain that quality of learning, that process, these developmental occasions at the hospital? We created in those six days what Donald Oliver and K. Waldron Gershman (1989) call an occasion of being and knowing.

This occurred for the twelve doctors in Bangladesh: they got out of their heads, freed somewhat from the abstractions of diarrhea as a disease and a research agenda. They moved into their hearts and hands. The question all adult educators face is this: How can we make these occasions occur regularly, with adequate rewards and systems for continuation, so that the work we do is accountable and learners know that they know?

Design Challenges

- What would you have done differently if you had arrived in Dacca, as I did, with the mandate to teach a group of physicians the elements of popular education in one week?

- What do you now understand by *immediacy*? By *engagement*? By *accountability*? How will you use these principles in your work?

- How can you change a course you are now teaching to make it more immediate for the learners? How can you win their deeper engagement? And how can you prove to yourself and to your adult learners that your teaching is accountable?

PART THREE:

Becoming an Effective Teacher of Adults

15

Using the Twelve Principles in Your Own Teaching

Having persevered this far through these tales and having done some of the design challenges, you are now familiar enough with these selected principles and practices of adult learning (popular education) to use them in your own designs. You probably recognize that you are already using many of them in your own teaching. As one group of adult educators in Chile told me: "We have been doing this for years. We just didn't know what to call it!" Knowing what to call the principles can be a guide to using them intentionally in all our adult learning designs.

While we honor the teaching style (that is, the personality) of each teacher, we also honor the transcendence of these principles. Adult educators will use these principles in their own way, reflecting their own teaching style. The principles remain the same. The characteristics of a particular group of learners are defined as we use the Seven Steps and begin with the Who. All our decisions about tasks and materials, sequence and reinforcement, evaluation and application, are informed by these data. Tasks appropriate for a group of twenty-five-year-old National Service recruits will not be effective with a group of senior citizens. Who the learners are makes a world of difference.

The Principles in Action

The twelve principles and practices we have focused on in these stories are: needs assessment; safety; sound relationships; sequence and reinforcement; praxis (action with reflection); respect for learners as subjects of their own learning; cognitive, affective, and psychomotor aspects of learning (ideas, feelings, actions); immediacy; clear roles; teamwork in small groups; engagement; and accountability. We have shown how the Seven Steps of Planning involve all of these principles and practices in the preparation of a learning design.

Needs Assessment

In your own programs, a needs assessment can be done in a variety of ways. If you are teaching young entrepreneurs how to start a business, how about a telephone survey of a sample of those registered for your course? In that survey you might ask: "What are your greatest fears? What are your hopes for your small business? What are the three areas you feel you need to learn about?" If you use a written survey, you can list all the potential content of your course and invite them to indicate which three items seem most important to them.

If you are teaching young people in college a life skill such as responsible parenting, this principle guides you in choosing how you will discover what they already know about this intimate subject and what they think they need to know for their own safety and personal development. Using a case study of a young couple making tough decisions about intimacy and marriage can enable the group of young learners to manifest and assess their own learning needs. As they analyze and do problem solving on a complex case, they show where their own knowledge is lacking and where they need to develop clearer attitudes about sensitive issues. This case study can be a part of the learning design, or it can be used prior to the session. Needs assessment is a continuous process: we discover learners' needs, we meet them, and in doing so through engaging tasks we discover further needs.

Here is a final example of needs assessment from the field. Suppose you are teaching organic gardening to an avid group of men and women who want to raise vegetables for their own families. How do you know what they need to know? Ask them! Study their experience and their educational profile! Observe them in the garden! How about going to the homes of a small sample of the group to see how they have set up their family vegetable gardens? (If you came to mine, you would immediately discover a great deal that I obviously need to know.) Designing innovative ways to do these three needs assessment tasks—ask, study, observe—is your constant challenge as an educator using this popular education approach to learning.

Safety

Establishing an environment of safety in the setting of the learning and in the process, for both learners and teacher, is both essential and challenging. Let's look at a National Service program where young adults come to learn how to offer technical services to a community, and work together as a team. How can we assure they will feel safe enough in this venture to stay with it, to do the job well, and to be creative and critical in their response to the program? Other principles and practices come in here: affirmation, listening, echoing their words and feelings, a sequence of learning tasks that is feasible and developmental, respect for them as subjects of their own lives and learning, clear roles, and accountability of leaders to the learners and to the program. Safety can be *felt* in a learning situation. These are the signs: laughter, a certain ease and camaraderie, a flow of questions from the learners, the teacher's invitation for comments on the process.

In a graduate course at the University of North Carolina School of Public Health, for example, the graduate students feel the safety I am trying to establish when they are invited to list their expectations of the course in light of the set objectives. I always tell them I will try to model the principles and practices of popular education I am teaching, and I invite their comments on that effort. By the fourth week of every semester, and only in the fourth week, a graduate student will question my decision to do something or will ask why I said what I said. It takes time for roles to change and for safety to work its magic toward honest dialogue.

Imagine the possibilities for such honest dialogue in an orientation program for new employees, or a training program for police officers, or firefighters, or nursing assistants. Again, the establishment of an environment of safety for oneself and the learners is part and parcel of preparing an effective learning design.

Sound Relationships

A relationship of mutual respect between teacher and learner is often cited as the most important motivator of adult learners. There are many ways a teacher can develop this relationship.

In a course on English as a second language, the instructor invites learners to call him Mr. Jones and says he will call them by whatever name they wish. As each person says his or her name, the instructor writes it on the board in large letters (even though he has a registration list). He then greets the learner, using the name the learner has suggested. "Good evening, Miss Lao."

In a community college woodworking class, the instructor gives the group his telephone number and invites them to call him whenever they're concerned about what they are doing in their home woodworking shops. This creates a sound relationship between learner and teacher, as the learner recognizes that the teacher is an available resource.

A physician working with a pregnant woman who is somewhat frightened of all the testing facing her can develop this sound relationship for learning by gently explaining the tests, inviting questions, and even accompanying the woman with her spouse to the first test. Developing such a relationship takes time. Without that investment of time, however, the woman will perceive the physician as a technician, not a teacher.

Sequence and Reinforcement

How often must a skill or concept or attitude be practiced in order for it to be known? In our Jubilee Introduction to Popular Education workshops, which are intensive week-long courses, we find the adult learners need maximum amounts of reinforcement before they are able to design a session using these principles and practices. In the past we would set them to this task in teams so early that we almost always met resistance of one kind or another. Now, having learned by our mistakes, we work with them through a gentle set of well-sequenced tasks, reinforcing their skills in using the Seven Steps of Planning, in designing an achievement-based objective, in setting an engaging learning task with clear resource materials, and in evaluating the immediate learning. Participants do this once, review it, and then do it again, and again, and again. After ten times, by George, they've got it!

We have learned that the design of learning tasks must reflect an appropriate sequence for the group plus adequate reinforcement. Parents learning together how to care for their new infant need such learning tasks monitored by a nurse or assistant, sequenced to move from simple and safe to complex, repeated until they indeed know they know. Their feeling of safety in the skill or with the knowledge is clearly manifest when they have had time to repeat a task or practice a skill.

New employees learning to work a complicated machine need to do the job with a mentor in small, well-sequenced tasks, then repeat it with guidance, then solo, again and again. Their smile of confidence and their agility with a complex series of maneuvers will be indicator enough that they know they know. Coaching is never telling. It is setting out a well-sequenced series of small tasks, repeating them often enough, and affirming the learners as they show their new skills. While such an effort seems to involve more time than the instructors can afford, it can save time and money in the long run. Learners will know their jobs and will work with confidence. We have an axiom: the more competent the teaching (with sequence and reinforcement), the more capable the worker and the less time lost in correction and reteaching.

Praxis: Action with Reflection

As we reinforce a skill, we might invite a learner to practice it. Praxis—action with reflection—is more than practice. It means, as we have seen, that the learner does what she is learning and immediately reflects upon that doing.

How does one "do" a new concept? If you were teaching new entrepreneurs how to keep their accounts, there are many concepts you would use: balance of expenses and income; debits and credits; deductible and nondeductible items. The learning tasks you set for them can be applications of these concepts. As learners completed each learning task, your next open question could be: "How did you use the concept of balance in this task?" That is praxis: action with reflection.

When adults begin to learn how to use a computer and programs, praxis is vital. Simple tasks using concepts such as macros, hot keys, saving, formatting, and the skills related to each can be set in an appropriate sequence with adequate reinforcement. Then as each task is done, the concept or skill is made explicit through an open question: "What macro was most useful to you in this task? Which hot key did you use? What is your common way of saving a file?" That is praxis: action with reflection. When we consciously use praxis in our design of learning tasks, the learners begin asking us questions—thinking critically not only about the content but also about the process.

Respect for Learners

No matter what you do, adult learners will learn what they need and want to know. This is at once a consoling and a challenging thought. Our task is to show, in every way possible, our respect for the learners as subjects or decision makers of their own learning. I have an axiom: "Do not tell what you can ask. Do not ask if you know the answer; tell in dialogue." This invites the adult educator to honor the learner first as an adult with years of experience and informal as well as formal learning. Tapping this experience is one way to show respect. Inviting people to tell their stories, to share their hopes and fears, to simply express their expectations of an educational event, is a way to show this respect for them as subjects of their own lives as well as of their own learning.

Literacy classes for the homeless are now part of the adult basic skills program of many states. In North Carolina, this program is managed through the community colleges. How can instructors design ways to demonstrate their respect for these learners who must practice being subjects of their own learning in this single, small area of their troubled lives? I have seen instructors invite homeless learners to tell the story of their best day, their worst night, their dream job. I have heard the poems of homeless literacy students invited by an instructor to tell their story in song or verse. Listening to learners' stories of their lives, their families, their hopes and dreams is a way of showing respect for them as subjects.

In a training course the mere invitation to learners to express their hopes and fears about the course, to name their expectations, is a simple way of showing respect and listening to them acting as subjects of their own learning. We may not be able to meet their expectations. That is not the issue. The issue is to listen. Then we can list the resources adults can use to meet the needs they have cited.

Ideas, Feelings, Actions

We have seen through these tales of learning and teaching the consistent use of three aspects of popular education: the cognitive (ideas); the affective (feelings); the psychomotor (actions). Here is a principle we can put to immediate use as we design training or adult learning. How is my teaching involving the learner in thinking, feeling, and doing? Where is the cognitive material in my content? Where is the affective? Where are the psychomotor aspects of the learning tasks I set?

A simple class in nutrition at a clinic can readily employ all these aspects if this principle is honored. The learners may read a story and see a picture of a hungry child. They may have been asked to bring to the class a small piece of food from their homes. The instructor adds other foods to the table, and the learners are invited to prepare, from all these foods, a simple meal for this child. I have a poignant memory of a day in a Caribbean country where a nurse, using her university training in nutrition education, stood in the shade of a mango tree that was dripping with ripe, mouth-watering mangoes, teaching a group of mothers how to feed their children. The nurse wanted to make the point that fruit was important in the diet of children and infants. She had a series of large posters that she showed the women—pictures of mangoes and other fruit. Her lecture went on and on, the women dozed, their children squirmed in their arms. Perhaps, if she had known about the importance of this threefold set of learning factors, she might have had the mothers pick a mango, peel it, and eat it with their children. Her point would have been made as she invited reflection on that juicy experience with the learners. It could have been a moment of sweet praxis!

So much of our own education dealt with cognitive matter, without consideration of affective or psychomotor aspects, that it is a great temptation to *tell* people what they need or want to know. Setting achievement-based objectives in our designs and learning tasks, as we plan the program, can help us recall and use this important principle of popular education. As Kurt Lewin (1951) puts it, learning is more effective when it is an active rather than a passive process.

Immediacy

In Chapter Two, I showed an example of a training course for National Service staff where immediacy was operative. You apply this principle every time you see adult learners using what you have taught and celebrating the usefulness of it. In both formal and non-formal education, immediacy is a key motivator.

Coaching adults in their development of trade skills of any kind involves this principle. You invite them to use the first section of a skill, celebrate that, reflect on the process, and move on to the next part. The immediate success encourages the learners to begin to believe they can learn.

In a statistics course at a local university, a gifted teacher has a programmed approach to the concepts, skills, and attitudes she is teaching. That is, through learning tasks she teaches one intro-ductory skill and concept. As learners use it, they find it applicable to their daily life and try it at home. They come back to class excited and motivated to learn the next complex concept or skill. This teacher is conscious of the principle of immediacy: the need of adult learners to be able to use what they are learning.

In a program on substance abuse in a community setting, the men and women tell their stories of the destructiveness of their addictive habit. They do not urge their colleagues to abstain, but the immediacy of the story moves all who hear it. It is as if the lis-teners live vicariously the pain and fear of the storyteller. There is powerful immediacy in these programs.

Retraining men and women for new skills demands this prin-ciple too. Unless adults see that their efforts are having practical and immediate results, they rarely continue in a retraining program. Doing such a skill-based program in a setting where jobs requiring the new skill are available is a cogent application of the principle of immediacy.

Clear Roles

Every adult educator who has tried to use a participative approach has stories to tell about the difficulty caused by confusion of roles. Who is the decision maker about what is taught in an adult learn-ing situation? Who therefore has a deliberative voice? Who can offer suggestions about the content of a course, the processes being used, or the time arrangements? Who therefore has a consultative voice?

Teaching adults to use new farm machinery that will increase the productivity of their land is a common agricultural extension effort. The role of the extension agent is manifold: technician, adviser, resource person, coach, evaluator. Some of these roles may be shared by learners as people work in small groups or teams. Some of these roles change as the learners become more proficient in the skill. In a popular education setting where dialogue is occurring, the agent will herself take a learning role as she listens to the questions and suggestions of the farmers. What this principle stresses is that the roles must be clear and ambiguity must be avoided. If farmers see the agent as the decision maker about what type of new machines they should purchase for their farms—and that is not the agent's role at all—this point needs to be clarified.

In teaching teachers to use the principles and practices of popular education, we at Jubilee often speak of ourselves as future resources. Students can call us at any time to review a program or locate a missing reference. However, if students see us as those who will design their programs for them, they need to be told very clearly that they are wrong. Clarity of role is the issue here.

Teamwork in Small Groups

Teamwork is as much a practice as a principle of popular education. Many of the stories in this book refer to teamwork and work in small groups. We have an axiom at Jubilee: a learning task is an open question put to a small group with the resources they need to respond to it. Even when working with a large group of adults, we can use small groups and teams to do certain learning tasks. In training men and women for a particular trade, practice in skills can be accomplished in small groups for reinforcement, feedback, and efficient learning. I have "taught" audiences of over a thousand people, asking them to turn to their neighbors, make small groups for themselves, and do a learning task. The energy released when men and women do such a task is surprising.

Teaching adults how to invest their resources, how to purchase a home, how to select a useful and durable vehicle, we can invite them to work together on learning tasks and watch the peer education, group bonding, and learning that occur. Individual efforts at learning are sometimes necessary. But pitting individuals against one another in a destructive competition is not acceptable in popular education. We live and learn together.

Engagement

Without engagement there is no learning. We know this from our own learning experience. The protocols of formal learning, however, put the burden of engagement on the learner. In popular education we accept that our designs, based on a competent needs assessment, can be engaging and, therefore, help adults learn. If we accept that a learning task is an open question put to a small group with the materials and resources they need to respond, we know how to engage learners. All the successful educational programs you have designed, taught, and celebrated in your life were those in which learners were deeply engaged.

Efforts to cover a set curriculum often lead to neglect of this principle of engagement. Our job in adult education is not to cover a set of course materials, but to engage adults in effective and significant learning. As community banks educate more families about alternatives to funding the purchase of a home or a vehicle, or the kinds of investments they can make, the engagement of these men and women in this learning as active subjects—or decision makers—is vital. They have important questions to ask about their land, their rights, and their responsibilities as they face the first mortgage of their lives. Bankers, in turn, have much to learn from such an engaging dialogue with these clients.

Accountability

How do they know they know? This is the accountability question that reaches back to touch all the other principles and practices. Each of the stories portrays our efforts to make the educational event accountable to the learners. One's first experience of this mutual accountability can be shocking. We may suddenly stop in the midst of a workshop and say: "Wait! A lot of us are having trouble with this. Let's form small groups to work it through once more with feeling." To those who apparently comprehend a concept or skill or attitude we may say: "You five each get a small group around you to work on this problem, and let me know what I can do to help. We are not leaving this item until I'm convinced that you all know you know!"

Honest Dialogue

Paulo Freire describes how in a dialogue approach to adult learning the teacher learns and the learner teaches. I trust this was obvious in all the stories. My colleagues and I learned at least as much as any of the participants. A story from my Tanzanian experience makes this clear: We were teaching a group of church teachers at a distant parish. My colleague had gone into town for supplies, and I was leading the session on a hot afternoon. The men, all in their thirties and forties, got into a jolly mood. They began acting quite frivolous, laughing and telling jokes during the learning tasks. I lost my temper and in an unlikely outburst said to these adults: "Please, you've got to get serious about this work! This workshop has cost a lot of money! We've got to get down to business."

I knew from the silence that filled that room that I had stepped outside all bounds of propriety. At least I had the good grace to keep still as Tomas got up to say to his fellows, "I am going to get the afternoon bus home! What Jane has said has cut me to the heart." One by one the men got up and each had a word to say to me. They were polite and quiet. One said, "I may look poor, but when you come to my village you will see houses that I have built, and a farm that I plow, and a family of many children. That is my wealth!"

At one point during the declamations, my colleague arrived on the scene. I motioned to her to sit down. She heard all of this and wondered what in the world had happened. I did have the good grace to sit still, keep quiet, and pay attention. When they finished, they were standing with their hand on the door and I said, in a choked voice, "Gentlemen, I have been teaching in Tanzania for almost twenty years. No one has ever spoken to me with this kind of honesty before. I had no idea of the significance of what I said. I apologize sincerely and I thank you for your honesty."

The group of adult men looked at one another, smiled at the two of us, and sat down. They moved back to the task at hand very naturally until they were interrupted by Tomas who stood up again to announce, "I just want to say I am not taking that two o'clock bus home!"

When adult students ask me about the best learning experience in my life, I usually tell that story. Julius Nyerere, philosopher-president of Tanzania, said that he wanted the nation to grow out of its own roots. This is true not only for nations but for individuals. As we search for principles and practices of adult learning, of popular education, that might apply in diverse situations, we educators must celebrate our own ability to listen, to learn, to grow out of our own roots.

16

How Do You Know You Know?

We know that merely reading a book does not often change behavior. But let us suppose that you have not read this book. You have never met Fatuma, or Jean Pierre, or the doctors of the International Center for the Control of Diarrheal Disease, or Durga. You have never heard of the Seven Steps of Planning or the principles of popular education.

Supposing

You have the occasion to plan a course for adult learners. What do you do? You probably consider what it is you want to teach them, organize that content into reasonable and cogent units, and give it to them, one way or another. You may use a video, or a lecture, or invite small-group discussions. You will probably not be aware that some of your questions are closed or that the sequence in your presentation is inappropriate. You may not recognize the need for reinforcement. You may struggle valiantly with the distance that separates you culturally, cognitively, by age, or by gender from the learners. You may not be aware that you are not using their generative themes and, therefore, your well-prepared content is lost on them. You probably did not do a learning needs assessment or ask the learners their expectations of the course. Since you did not use the Seven Steps of Planning, you have not been intentional about the time frame or the site of the course.

You probably do not know you need to work toward optimal dialogue about the content with the learners as subjects. You probably teach very well without recognizing that, often, the more teaching, the less learning. There are probably no learning tasks in your outline. Probably a lot of the work you do involves cognitive content without attention to the affective and psychomotor aspects. At the end of the course, you may use an evaluation instrument that measures their cognitive learning. You will probably not ask yourself: How do they know they know?

This book, therefore, could make a difference in your preparation, your teaching, and the means you choose to evaluate their learning. The mother of a dear friend recently described her first venture into the world of computers. She decided to take a continuing education course at a community college. She paid her tuition, purchased her textbook, and bravely entered the first class. She was surrounded by peers: other white-haired grandmothers who had finally recognized that they must breach the wall separating them from computer literacy. The young, enthusiastic teacher spent the first class preaching in a language my friend's mother could not understand: bits, bytes, RAM, CD-ROM! She waited for the moment when they would learn how to turn the computer on. It never came. After fifty minutes of listening to well-organized but incomprehensible teaching, she and many of her peers ran from the class, never to return. The world of computers is still a fearful unknown to these venturesome seniors. But suppose that young teacher had read this book. What a world of difference it might have made for those women.

Proposing

You have read this book. The Seven Steps of Planning are yours to use as you begin to design your course, training, orientation, workshop. Your efforts at dialogue through learning needs analysis, open questions, learning tasks, and qualitative evaluation invite adult learners to participate and examine the content you are teaching. As subjects of the learning, they argue and share their different values and perceptions with you in an exciting learning encounter.

Your learning tasks are cognitive, affective, and psychomotor. People are using all their senses, their potential for affect, and their muscles as they learn. They are doing it. And the immediacy of their learning motivates them to further examination and praxis.

Because you are using small groups, these adults are sharing their lives and value systems with one another, focused by the content they are learning together. They are, in fact, teaching one another. There is stimulating competition going on. The materials they are using reflect their own language and their own themes, which you heard during your learning needs assessment. Since your questions are mostly open, they recognize that your role is not only that of expert in this content area but also that of learner. The safety in the course invites some surprising questions from the adult learners—taking you all to levels of learning you may not have anticipated. You and they can celebrate the power of dialogue.

References

Adams, F. *Unearthing Seeds of Fire: The Idea of Highlander*. Mounteagle, Tenn.: John Blair, 1975.

Bloom, B. S. *Taxonomy of Educational Objectives*. New York: McKay, 1956.

Brookfield, S. *Adult Learners, Adult Education and the Community*. New York: Teachers College Press, 1984.

Brookfield, S. *Understanding and Facilitating Adult Learning: A Comprehensive Analysis of Principles and Effective Practices*. San Francisco: Jossey-Bass, 1986.

Brookfield, S. *Developing Critical Thinkers: Challenging Adults to Explore Alternative Ways of Thinking and Acting*. San Francisco: Jossey-Bass, 1987.

Brookfield, S. *The Skillful Teacher: On Technique, Trust, and Responsiveness in the Classroom*. San Francisco: Jossey-Bass, 1990.

Bryson, J. *Strategic Planning for Public and Nonprofit Organizations: A Guide to Strengthening and Sustaining Organizational Achievement*. San Francisco: Jossey-Bass, 1988.

Campbell, J. *Myths to Live By*. New York: Viking, 1972.

Campbell, J. *Changing Images of Man*. New York: Pergamon Press, 1982.

Campbell, J. *The Power of Myth*. New York: Doubleday, 1988.

Cardenal, F., and Miller, V. "Nicaragua 1980: The Battle of the ABCs." *Harvard Educational Review*, 1981, *51*(1), 9–29.

Freire, P. *Cultural Action for Freedom*. Monograph Series, no. 1. Cambridge, Mass.: Harvard Educational Review, 1970.

Freire, P. *Pedagogy of the Oppressed*. New York: Herder and Herder, 1972.

Freire, P. *The Politics of Education*. South Hadley, Mass.: Bergin & Garvey, 1985.

Freire, P., and Faundez, A. *Learning to Question: A Pedagogy of Liberation*. New York: Herder and Herder, 1972.

Freire, P., and Horton, M. *We Make the Road by Walking: Conversations on Education and Social Change*. Philadelphia: Temple University Press, 1990.

Freire, P., and Macedo, D. *Literacy: Reading the Word and the World*. New York: Bergin & Garvey, 1987.

Freire, P., and Shor, I. *A Pedagogy for Liberation: Dialogues on Transforming Education*. New York: Bergin & Garvey, 1987.

Hope, A., Timmel, S., and Hodzi, C. *Training for Transformation: A Handbook for Community Workers*. Harare, Zimbabwe: Mambo Press, 1984.

Hutchinson, T. "Community Needs Analysis Methodology." Unpublished paper, University of Massachusetts, 1978.

Johnson, D., and Johnson, F. *Joining Together: Group Theory and Group Skills*. Englewood Cliffs, N.J.: Prentice-Hall, 1991.

Jung, C. *The Collected Works*. Princeton: Princeton University Press, 1969.

Kindervatter, S. *Nonformal Education as an Empowering Process*. Amherst: Center for International Education, University of Massachusetts, 1979.

Knowles, M. *The Modern Practice of Adult Education: An Autobiographical Journey*. New York: Association Press, 1970.

Knowles, M. *Self-Directed Learning: A Guide for Learners and Teachers*. Chicago: Follett, 1975.

Knowles, M. *The Adult Learner: A Neglected Species*. Houston: Gulf, 1978.

Knowles, M. *The Making of an Adult Educator*. San Francisco: Jossey-Bass, 1989.

Knox, A. *Developing, Administering, and Evaluating Adult Education*. San Francisco: Jossey-Bass, 1980.

Knox, A. *Helping Adults Learn: A Guide to Planning, Implementing, and Conducting Programs*. San Francisco: Jossey-Bass, 1986.

Kuhn, T. *The Structure of Scientific Revolutions*. Chicago: University of Chicago Press, 1970.

Lazear, D. *Seven Ways of Knowing: Teaching for Multiple Intelligence*. Palatine, Ill.: Skylight Publishing, 1991.

Lewin, K. *Field Theory in Social Science*. New York: HarperCollins, 1951.

Maturana, H., and Varela, F. *The Tree of Knowledge*. Boston: Shambhala, 1992.

Memmi, A. *The Colonizer and the Colonized*. Boston: Beacon Press, 1965.

Oliver, D. *Education and Community*. Berkeley: McCutchan, 1976.

Oliver, D., with Waldron Gershman, K. *Education, Modernity and Fractured Meaning*. Albany: SUNY Press, 1989.

Schön, D. *Educating the Reflective Practitioner: Toward a New Design for Teaching and Learning in the Professions*. San Francisco: Jossey-Bass, 1987.

Shor, I. *Critical Teaching and Everyday Life*. Montreal: Black Rose Books, 1980.

Srinivasan, L. *Perspectives on Nonformal Adult Learning*. New York: World Education, 1977.

Srinivasan, L. *Options for Educators*. New York: PACT/CDS, 1992.

Svendsen, D., and Wijetilleke, S. *NAVAMAGA: Training Activities for Group Building, Health and Income Generation*. New York: Women, Ink, 1983.

Vella, J. *Learning to Listen*. Amherst: Center for International Development, University of Massachusetts, 1979.

Vella, J. *Learning to Teach*. New York: Women, Ink, 1989.

Vella, J. *Learning to Listen to Mothers*. Washington, D.C.: Academy for Educational Development, 1992.

Werner, D., and Bower, B. *Helping Health Workers Learn*. Palo Alto, Calif.: Hesperian Foundation, 1982.

Index